Teaching Scriptwriting, Screenplays and Storyboards for Film and TV Production

Series Editor: Vivienne Clark
Commissioning Editor: Wendy Earle

bfi Education

British Library Cataloguing-in-Publication Data
A catalogue record for this book is available in the British Library

ISBN 0851709745

First published in 2003 by the British Film Institute
21 Stephen Street, London W1T 1LN

Student worksheets to support this guide are supplied at: www.bfi.org.uk/tfms
User name: **scriptwriter**   Password: **te1510sc**

Design: Amanda Hawkes
Cover photographs: Courtesy of *bfi* Stills
Printed in Great Britain by Cromwell Press

www.bfi.org.uk

The British Film Institute gives everyone the opportunity to increase their understanding and
appreciation of film and television from around the world.

Contents

Introduction to the series

The recent rapid growth of both Film and Media Studies post-16 has inevitably led to a demand for more teachers of these popular courses. But, given the comparatively recent appearance of both subjects at degree level (and limited availability of relevant post-graduate teaching courses), many new and experienced teachers from other disciplines are faced with teaching either subject for the first time, without a degree-level background.

In addition, the new post-16 specifications saw the arrival of new set topics and areas of study, and some of the specifications have changing topics, so there is a pressing need for up-to-date resources to help teacher preparation.

This series has been developed with these factors – and the busy teacher – in mind. Each title aims to provide teachers with an accessible reference resource, with essential topic content, as well as clear guidance on good classroom practice to improve the quality of their teaching and learning. Every author in the series is an experienced practitioner of Film and/or Media Studies at this level and many have examining/moderating experience.

Key features:

- Assessment contexts
- Suggested schemes of work
- Historical contexts (where appropriate)
- Key facts, statistics and terms
- Detailed reference to the key concepts of Film and Media Studies
- Detailed case studies
- Glossaries
- Bibliographies
- Student worksheets, activities and resources (available online) – ready to print and photocopy for the classroom.

Other titles in the series include:

Teaching Scriptwriting, Screenplays and Storyboards; Teaching Digital Video Production; Teaching British Cinema since 1990; Teaching Television News; Teaching Film Language; Teaching Television Language; Teaching British Television since 1990; Teaching Film Censorship and Controversy; Teaching Women & Film; Teaching Video Games; Teaching World Cinema; Teaching Television Soap Opera.

SERIES EDITOR: Vivienne Clark is a former Head of Film and Media Studies. She is an Advanced Skills Teacher; Associate Tutor of the British Film Institute; and Principal Examiner for A level Media Studies for one of the English awarding bodies. She is a freelance teacher trainer and writer on Media and Film Studies, with several published textbooks and teaching resources. She is also a course tutor on the *bfi*/Middlesex University MA level module: An Introduction to Media Education (distance learning).

Author: James Baker is Head of Media Studies at Hurtwood House School in Surrey. He is also a senior examiner for OCR and a freelance writer on media education.

Introduction

Assessment context

	Awarding body & level	Subject	Unit code	Module/Topic
✓	WJEC AS Level	Film Studies	FS1	Making Meaning 1: Practical Approaches to Learning – Creative Work – screenplays/storyboards
✓	WJEC AS Level	Film Studies	FS1	Making Meaning 1: Written Analysis 1 (Macro – Narrative and Genre)
✓	WJEC A2 Level	Film Studies	FS4	Making Meaning 2: Practical Approaches to Learning – Creative Work – screenplays/storyboards
✓	OCR AS Level	Media Studies	2730	Foundation Production – video/film/TV pre-production
✓	OCR A2 Level	Media Studies	2733	Advanced Production – video/film/TV pre-production
✓	AQA AS Level	Media Studies	MED2	Practical Production – video/film/TV pre-production
✓	WJEC AS Level	Media Studies	ME3	Making Media Texts – video/film/TV pre-production
✓	SQA Advanced Higher	Media Studies	D334 13	Media Production – video

This pack is also relevant to the teaching of practical media production assessments (film/TV/video) in the following specifications, as well as for Lifelong Learning and international courses:

- OCR – GNVQ and AVCE
- Ed-Excel – GNVQ and AVCE
- BTech National Diploma

This pack is also useful for anyone wanting to teach the narrative structure of films in a more practical way.

Why teach screenwriting and storyboards?

Media production work is now firmly entrenched in the Film and Media Studies curriculum and takes the form of accredited coursework in many post-16 specifications. Storyboards, scripts and screenplay extracts are increasingly common as coursework artefacts and are also frequently required as evidence of planning and preparation for audiovisual products.

As preparatory work, these activities can be neglected; the expertise of students and teachers, along with the benefits of affordable, sophisticated digital technology, means that many of the video artefacts being produced are of a seductively high technical quality. It is also often the case that less emphasis is placed on the activities of scripting and storyboarding than on the finished products. Sometimes, where storyboards and scripts are required, they are 'retro-fitted' to the artefact – fulfilling obligations to examination specifications, but otherwise pointless. Understandably the demands of time and volume reduce the perceived importance of these activities if they are not to be submitted as final products in their own right. However, they can make an enormous difference to the quality of the actual final products.

In addition, given that students tend to be required to produce extracts from notional works, rather than the works in their entirety, it can be tempting merely to focus on aesthetic components in a vacuum without giving full consideration to the narrative context. This can produce results which may contain impressive elements, but which often resort to cliché and lack narrative coherence.

Consequently there are a number of arguments for working on screenplays and/or storyboards, whether they are final products or preparatory products, and this pack is designed to show how scriptwriting and storyboarding can be valuable not only in a production context (although this is the primary focus) but also as ways of engaging with key aspects of the media curriculum in illuminating ways, for example:

- **Narrative**

  - Progressing beyond structural reductions of narrative into debates around specific story construction;
  - Putting story design theory into practice.

- **Genre**

  - Making fine distinctions between structurally congruent narratives by understanding the specifics that generate difference.

- **Visual literacy**

  - Engaging practically with the process of meaning production through a visual medium;
  - Practising a wide and informed vocabulary of techniques.

- **Industrial context**

  - Analysing existing screenplays, especially different drafts, can reveal how the exigencies of production bodies and markets can determine the nature of a 'literary' work for the screen.

- **ICT**

  - Acquiring skills with specific software, from using word processing style sheets to sequencing images.

This kind of work is useful because looking at film narratives as 'stories' rather than merely vehicles for ideology can provide a refreshingly new perspective. This is not to say that ideological considerations should be ignored, but work on screenplays provides an opportunity to discuss the mechanics of storytelling in their own right and to acknowledge the pleasure for audiences of being told a good story well.

In addition, perhaps less obviously, learning the principles of screenwriting and how to implement them encourages skills of information management and organisation. One could argue that a student learning how to structure a linear arrangement of related incidents, episodes and events leading to a dramatic resolution is engaging in a task analogous to that of essay writing, which entails structuring a linear arrangement of related arguments, interpretations and evidence leading to a persuasive conclusion. At the very least it can be argued that the construction of a screenplay, which necessitates the coherent sequencing of interconnected events, is an activity which engenders logical thought processes, which might benefit other, more analytical activities.

It may also open up some Higher Education and career options that might not otherwise have been considered: students who discover or develop an aptitude for screenwriting and/or storyboarding may be able to gain access to courses or employment in this field. It can also provide a much needed creative outlet for those students who have strong narrative and visual ideas, but, for whatever reason, find that they cannot give satisfactory realisation to these ideas via cameras and editing equipment.

How to use this guide

This pack provides ways to examine the components of screenplays and storyboards, and suggests a series of stages leading to a final project. The aim is to enable students to combine these elements in finished products which are creatively informed as well as critically engaged.

- **Unit 1 – Essential terms and concepts** defines some terms, examines screenplay format and provides an overview of some of the influential literature on screenwriting.

- **Unit 2 – Screenplay basics** takes components of screenwriting, such as structure, causality and character, and offers examples for analysis, case studies and prescriptive writing exercises.

- **Unit 3 – Storyboard basics** takes components of storyboards, such as the format, the frame and the sequence and offers some prescriptive exercises.

- **Unit 4 – Planning a project** is structured around the stages of a notional project and suggests some exercises which may lead to a final script extract and/or storyboard.

The activities in Units 2 and 3 can be used sequentially, or not, as required. Unit 4, however, offers linear progression towards a final product.

The worksheets to support these exercises are available at www.bfi.org.uk/tfms. To access the pages, click on the title *Teaching Scriptwriting, Screenplays and Storyboards for Film and TV Production*, and when asked, enter username: **scriptwriter** and the password: **te1510sc**. If you have any problems, email: education.resources@bfi.org.uk.

Teaching tips and advice

For post-16 students, screenplay writing can be an enjoyable return to the activity of storytelling – something they may not have done for a few years. There is a caveat, however: whereas much practical media work is collaborative and involves the impersonal veneer of pastiche or generic convention, screenplay development (more so than storyboard development, where the emphasis tends to be on visual aesthetics) is a solitary activity. Students may use it as an opportunity to express personal concerns, fears and anxieties and thus may expose themselves to a greater degree. This means that any critical feedback may need to be handled with some sensitivity.

There are some principles which underpin all of the work in this pack:

- Final products are more likely to be successful if they are preceded by self-contained prescriptive exercises which develop specific skills.
- Unthreatening, confidence-building exercises are necessary to create a supportive environment for sharing and discussing creative ideas.
- Regular formative assessment is essential (and can take a variety of forms, such as self and peer assessment as well as teacher assessment) in order to ensure that students do not feel 'caught out' by a final summative assessment and also to provide regular feedback.
- Whatever work is undertaken, it is essential that all students acquire a secure sense of what the project requires and what the assessment criteria are.
- Conventional work is usually more successful than experimental work. Some students may have fantastic, groundbreaking ideas, but these will not necessarily become effective vehicles to demonstrate their engagement with key aspects of film form.
- The most effective scripts maximise the potential of and demonstrate understanding of the medium; four pages of dialogue in a room doesn't necessarily provide much evidence that a student understands the potential of film to create meaning visually.
- Similarly, the most effective storyboards use, for example, different shot types, continuity, juxtapositions, and detailed information on sound and duration, in order to bring a sequence of static images to life.

While the creative dimension is crucial to this work, it is important that we recognise that we are not simply assessing good ideas, but the command and application of a range of skills designed to tell a story in an effective way for a specific medium. It is even more important that we are explicit about our criteria. Therefore it is essential that we supply our students with assessment criteria (from the specification) at the outset of the project. Collecting graded work from previous cohorts of students to use as examples is also recommended practice.

The following films and television programmes are referred to in this pack:

- *Friends*, Season 2, Episode 21
- *Joyride* (Jim Gillespie, UK, 1995)
- *Groundhog Day* (Harold Ramis, US, 1993)
- *The Full Monty* (Peter Cattaneo, US, 1997)
- *Fargo* (Joel and Ethan Coen, US, 1996)
- *Good Will Hunting* (Gus Van Sant, US, 1997)
- *Buffy the Vampire Slayer*, Season 2, Episode 2.

All of these are easily available through video retailers, except *Joyride* which may be ordered from *bfi* Education. See: www.bfi.org.uk/tfms for details.

Schemes of work

1. Screenplay structure

This six-week block has been designed as an introduction to basic story concepts and screenplay structure. It can be used to prepare for practical work in screenplay writing and storyboarding but could also be integrated into work on genre, given the extent to which generic differentiation depends upon variations in narrative elements of disruption and resolution.

Aims: To understand:

- Story concepts such as set-up, confrontation and resolution;
- Three Act Structure and causality;
- The concept of the Plot Point;
- The relationship between genre and types of resolution.

Outcomes:

- Close analysis of stories in different forms;
- Production of story outlines based on a character and a genre.

Week 1   Introduction to 'story'.

Brainstorm: 'What is a story?' and 'What makes a 'good' story?'

Analysis of *The Slave and the Lion* (Worksheet 3) – discussion of set up, confrontation, resolution and introduction to the protagonist's journey.

Predictive exercise – gradual screening of *Friends* (Worksheet 4, Activity 1).

Substitution exercise – *Friends* (Worksheet 4, Activity 2).

Discussion of genre – how different types of resolution might be effected in the *Friends* scenario in different genres.

Week 2   Practical group exercise – 'Consequences' (Worksheet 5) – building narrative outlines from a set-up.

Screening – *Joyride* or comparable short film – detailed consideration of causality, theme and Three Act Structure (Worksheet 6, Activities 1-3).

Group research performing similar analysis of other short films.

Week 3　Group presentations following research.

Discussion of Parker's ten story types and McKee's six plot types.

Categorisation exercise based on the above story types in relation to films included in group presentations (Worksheet 7).

Week 4　Screening – *Groundhog Day*.

Analysis of Three Act Structure and Plot Points in *Groundhog Day* (Worksheet 8).

- Follow up discussion of alternative Plot Points.
- A question of genre – categorisation of *Groundhog Day* in at least two different ways with detailed justification using textual evidence (essay or research and presentations).

Week 5　Discussion of different character types from examples already examined.

Analysis of character introductions from existing screenplays (Worksheet 9).

Small group exercise – construction of a character introduction (Worksheet 10).

Presentation of character introductions and discussion of results.

Week 6　Practical group exercise – based on a genre and a protagonist (possibly from previous activity), develop story outline to include identification of Plot Points and description of events in each act (Worksheet 20).

Presentation and evaluation of story proposals.

2. Storyboard production

This six-week block is designed to develop visual awareness and the specific skills connected with storyboard production. It incorporates some prescriptive sketching and sequencing exercises, covers story and genre, and results in a final original product.

Aims: To understand

- Terminology relating to shot type and movement;
- The generation of meaning through *mise en scène*;
- The generation of meaning through sequencing.

And to

- Acquire and practise skills in storyboard artistry.

Outcomes:

- Close analysis of shot types and sequences;
- Production of controlled storyboard sequences;
- Production of a storyboard extract.

Week 1   Introduction to basic shot types and simple sketching techniques (Worksheet 15, Activity 1).

Introduction to glossary of key technical terms and demonstration of how to represent movement in storyboards.

Representation of movement within a shot and of the camera (Worksheet 15, Activity 2).

Construction of a 10-shot storyboard sequence from a given list of prescribed shots. (Worksheet 15, Activity 3).

Week 2   *Mise en scène* analysis of moving image sequences (eg opening of *Taxi Driver*, 'stalking scene' from *Tightrope*) to illustrate significance of position, movement, lighting and framing.

Sketching exercise – replicating key shots from examples analysed.

Group exercise – construction of 20-shot storyboard sequence form a list of prescribed shots (Worksheet 16).

Week 3   Presentation of storyboard sequences (possibly on OHTs) and discussion of successful and less successful aspects. Comparison with *Buffy* extract (especially if storyboard is realised on video).

Examination of 'cross-cut' sequence from appropriate film or TV programme and discussion of tempo and framing.

Small group exercise – storyboard 10 to 15 shot sequence cutting between two locations and creating suspense (Worksheet 17).

Week 4   Presentation of sequences, and discussion focusing on duration, framing and sequencing.

Examination of existing storyboard example (eg *Alien*, *Mission to Mars*) – identification of techniques, conventions and effects discussed previously.

Genre recognition based on single frames – key visual conventions in examples.

Small group exercise – produce single frames which evoke generic associations (eg horror, western, noir).

Week 5   Brief introduction to Three Act Structure (Worksheet 4)

Practical group exercise – based on a genre and a protagonist, develop story outline to include description of key story events and resolution (Worksheet 18).

Presentation and evaluation of story proposals.

Week 6   Group exercise – selection of key sequence from story outline and consideration of how to represent it visually (Worksheet 22).

Pitch visual ideas for sequence – evaluate in the light of feedback.

Produce storyboard extract (Worksheet 22, Activity 2).

'Carousel' activity to get peer feedback on storyboard.

1

Essential terms and concepts

Terminology

Firstly it is worth clarifying some of the terms used in the title of this pack.

'Screenplay' tends to be used to refer to a script for a film of any length (although if it is for a short film this may be abbreviated to 'short', as in 'Sci-Fi Shorts'). 'Script', not 'screenplay', usually refers to scripts for most TV works (sitcoms and soaps, for example). Phil Parker in *The Art and Science of Screenwriting*, however, defines the term screenplay as:

> 'a television script, a commercial's script, a documentary script, a feature film screenplay or even notes on a possible set of images and sounds'

and coins the term 'screenwork' to describe

> 'any completed translation of a screenplay into a format which is watched/ experienced on a screen.' (p10)

Nevertheless, in an industrial context, the term 'screenplay' is generally understood to refer to a fictional work, a self-contained film narrative probably intended for theatrical exhibition. The term 'teleplay' can be used to differentiate a work for television from a screenplay, although this tends to be used in the US rather than the UK.

The term, 'scriptwriting', tends to be used to refer to the practice of writing for film, television and, to a degree, radio, but less so the theatre; the term tends to be applied to writing for a visual mass medium.

This pack focuses primarily on screenplays because much post-16 media production work tends to be concerned with the fictional products of the film industry, but it also examines examples from television in order to illustrate formal aspects of narrative construction.

In short then, this pack examines scriptwriting for both film and television only in as much as they illuminate the nature of screenplays; specific skills, such as writing for sitcoms or soaps, or writing jokes, fall beyond its remit.

Screenplay format

If students are submitting screenplays as final products, presentation is important. Scripts should be, at least, formatted with consistency and, at best, should follow industry conventions. Even if the script is not the final product, it is still worth encouraging students to format their scripts correctly. There are at least two advantages: the scripts become both much more useful as working documents and much clearer as supporting documents.

There are various software packages on the market dedicated to screenwriting. Some, such as *Dramatica Pro* and *StoryView*, are designed to assist with the process of story construction and others, such as *Movie Magic Screenwriter 2000* and *Final Draft* (the market leader) are designed to format scripts professionally. These packages are expensive, but there are some freeware options, such as *Rough Draft* (http://www.rsalsbury.co.uk/rd.htm).

However, perhaps the best option is to set up a template and styles in *Microsoft Word* which replicate professionally formatted scripts. This automates specific formatting processes, such as indenting, spacing and capitalisation, and assigns the operations to specific shortcut keys.

While there are some differences in format conventions between countries, and institutions, these are the key requirements:

- Clarity/ease of reading;
- The need for margins so that text is not obscured/obliterated by binding;
- The need for the different components of a script to be clearly differentiated;
- The need for a page of script to represent (approximately) one minute of screen time (hence the use of 12pt Courier – a mono-spaced font in a standardised size).

The model outlined below meets these requirements and uses the following conventions and components, which are typical for English language film and TV drama scripts.

The following notes are available on a student handout (Worksheet 1) at www.bfi.org.uk/tfms.

Scene: Screenplays are divided into scenes. (This is a technical definition, rather than the dramatic definition Robert McKee describes in *Story* which he also calls a 'story event'.) A scene can be defined as a unit of dramatic action which takes place in a specific location in continuous time.

Slug line or scene heading, eg EXT. MARTHA'S HOUSE. NIGHT: This tells us whether the scene is inside or outside, where it is and whether it's day or night. If more information about the location is needed it can go from the general to the specific or vice versa, eg INT. JACK'S CAR. HIGH STREET. DAY.

Scene direction: Always written in the present tense, this contains descriptions of the characters' actions and events relevant to the story. Characters' names are usually capitalised, eg

```
JACK notices MARTHA standing at the side of
the road. He slams the brakes on and the car
screeches to a halt.
```

Character cue: The name of the character who speaks. Always capitalised and centred above their speech.

Actor direction: In brackets under the character's name, used to describe the way, or to whom, they speak. Mostly redundant, and disliked by actors, but can be useful if the manner of speaking contradicts what appears to be the meaning or if there is potential uncertainty about who is being addressed.

Dialogue: What the characters say.

Camera shots and angles should not appear in the screenplay (although some writer/directors writing for themselves will include them).

It is worth looking at some real examples of formatted scripts when setting up templates in order to get a sense of what the finished product should look like. Unfortunately most examples of published scripts have been re-formatted to fit the space and dimensions of a paperback book, but many of the online scripts at 'script-o-rama' (http://www.script-o-rama.com) are formatted correctly and it should be possible to get some examples from film and TV production companies or even buy some.

A page of a screenplay which uses standard formatting, such as the one on the opppsite page, can be examined and discussed in relation to the 'naming of parts' process above and this will provide preparation for the simple formatting exercise described in Unit 2.

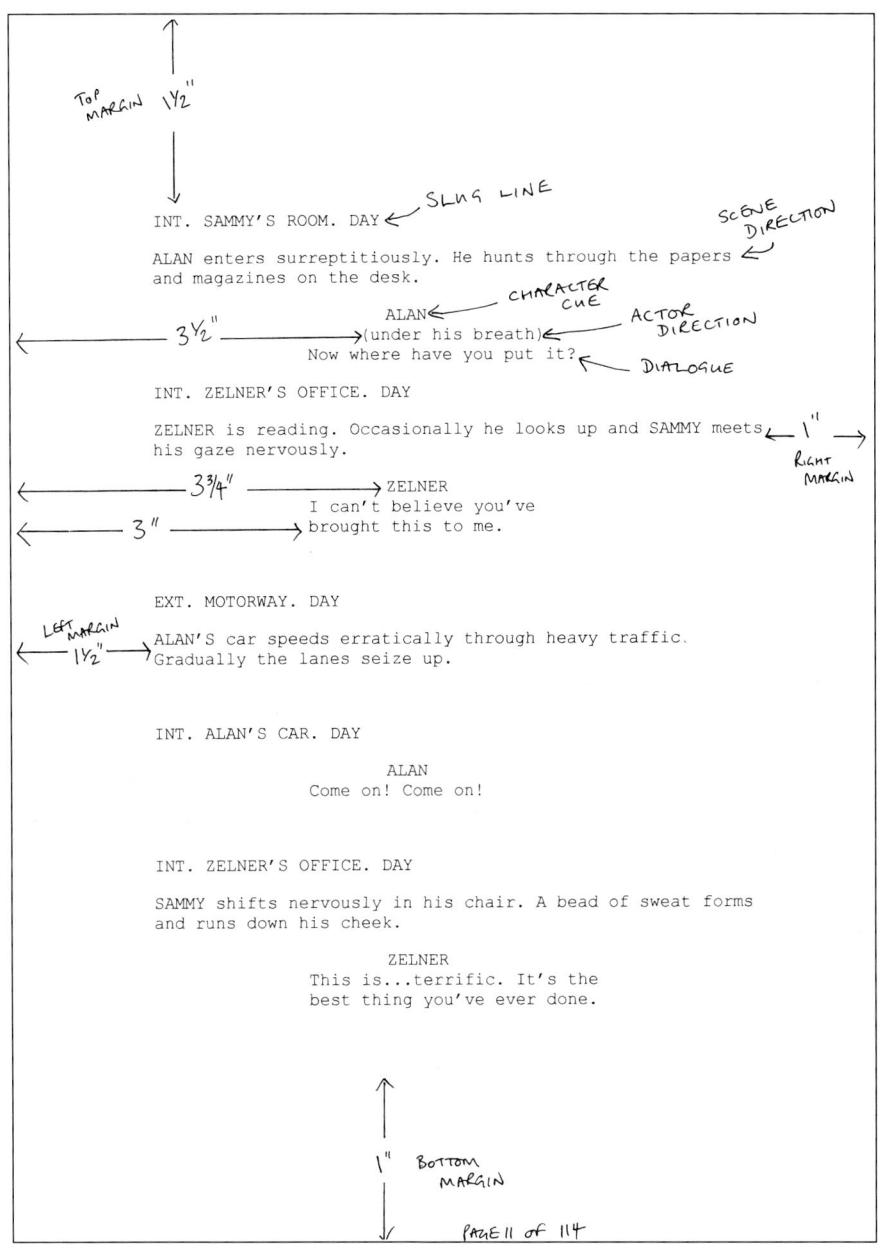

TOP MARGIN 1½"

INT. SAMMY'S ROOM. DAY ← SLUG LINE

SCENE DIRECTION

ALAN enters surreptitiously. He hunts through the papers ←
and magazines on the desk.

CHARACTER CUE

ALAN ←
3½" →(under his breath)← ACTOR DIRECTION
Now where have you put it? ← DIALOGUE

INT. ZELNER'S OFFICE. DAY

ZELNER is reading. Occasionally he looks up and SAMMY meets ← 1"
his gaze nervously.

RIGHT MARGIN

3¾" → ZELNER
I can't believe you've
3" → brought this to me.

EXT. MOTORWAY. DAY

LEFT MARGIN 1½"
ALAN'S car speeds erratically through heavy traffic.
Gradually the lanes seize up.

INT. ALAN'S CAR. DAY

ALAN
Come on! Come on!

INT. ZELNER'S OFFICE. DAY

SAMMY shifts nervously in his chair. A bead of sweat forms
and runs down his cheek.

ZELNER
This is...terrific. It's the
best thing you've ever done.

1" BOTTOM MARGIN

PAGE 11 of 114

This script page is available on a student handout (Worksheet 1) at
www.bfi.org.uk/tfms.

Three Act Structure:
An overview of screenwriting theory

There is a whole industry now dedicated to screenwriting – a multitude of books, magazines, courses, software packages and websites offer guidance to would-be professional writers.

The screenwriting books on the market essentially attempt to communicate to the aspiring screenwriter what makes a good story and how to tell that story. Some emphasise the mechanics, the craft of screenwriting, others stress the need for the writer to develop as an artist and some persuade us that stories are widely understood through shared archetypes. They are all, to varying degrees, predicated on the notion that a 'good story' is universal and that, although some are blessed with the talent to do it instinctively, it is possible, through investigation of the form, to acquire the necessary techniques.

It is useful for teachers to have access to some of these texts for reference and, although they may be a bit daunting for many students, they would be of interest to those who are particularly creative and motivated – especially those producing screenplays for AS/A level Film Studies.

Below are summaries of some of the key texts which have informed, and continue to inform, contemporary screenwriting.

● Syd Field, *Screenplay*

First published in 1979, and for some time *the* scriptwriter's bible, *Screenplay* is a practical 'how to' book from a Hollywood insider with experience of screenwriting, script reading, producing, consulting and teaching. Field takes a practical approach to the craft of screenwriting and insists that his book will 'enable the reader to sit down and write a screenplay from the position of choice, confidence and security.' (p5)

Central to *Screenplay* is the concept of the Three Act Structure – the paradigm (based on a two-hour/120-page Hollywood film) which Field argues is fundamental to a successful screenplay and which comprises:

Act I: Set-up, 'a unit of dramatic action that is approximately 30 pages long' in which 'the story, the characters, the dramatic premise, the situation … the relationships between the main character and the other people who inhabit the landscape of his or her world' are all established. (p10)

Act II: Confrontation, 'a unit of dramatic action that is approximately 60 pages long' in which 'the main character encounters obstacle after obstacle after obstacle that keeps him from achieving his or her dramatic need.' (p11)

Act III: Resolution, 'a unit of dramatic action that goes from the end of Act II, approximately page 90, to the end of the screenplay' which 'resolves the story.' (p12)

Field uses this schematic, perhaps even mechanical, model to argue how the writer must create the transitions between acts through the use of 'Plot Points' – 'a Plot Point is any incident, episode, or event that "hooks" into the action and spins it around into another direction.' (p115)

PLOT POINT I

Field says that Plot Point I should occur at the end of Act I and uses examples from *Chinatown* (Roman Polanski, US, 1974) and *Witness* (Peter Weir, US, 1985) to illustrate it:

- In *Chinatown* 'the arrival of the real Mrs. Mulwray is what "hooks" into the action and spins it around into Act II. Jake Gittes must find out who set him up, and why. It happens at about page 23.' (p13)
- In *Witness*, when John Book has reached an investigative impasse, the boy Samuel points at a picture in a newspaper article in a trophy cabinet. 'Book nods his head in understanding. He knows who the murderer is. Now he has to bring him to justice. It is Plot Point I. It occurs on page 25 of the screenplay.' (p13)

PLOT POINT II

This Plot Point functions in a similar way, but spins the action around into Act III. Field argues that 'it usually occurs at about page 85 or 90 of the screenplay' and uses moments from the two films above as examples:

- In *Chinatown*, Plot Point II is when Gittes 'finds a pair of horn-rimmed glasses in the pond where Hollis Mulwray was murdered and knows they belong to Mulwray, or to the person who killed him. This leads to the resolution of the story.' (p14)
- In *Witness*, Field suggests that 'after Book learns that his partner has been killed, he knows it's time to go back to Philadelphia and bring the guilty policemen to justice' and that this, therefore, constitutes Plot Point II, as it precipitates the final act shoot out between them all.

The waters are muddied slightly when Field suggests that

> 'when your screenplay is completed, it may contain as many as 15 plot points. How many you have … depends upon your story. Each plot point moves the story forward, toward the resolution' (p115)

However, he is clear and insistent that the key Plot Points are the ones which precipitate Act II and Act III respectively. He argues that these are the anchors of the story and that, before one begins to write, one must know four things: the ending, the beginning, the plot point at the end of Act I and the Plot Point at the end of Act II.

Essentially this book is about how to tell stories for the screen in such a way that they stand a good chance of being successful Hollywood movies. Criticisms might be that it is a prescriptive, formulaic approach to a creative activity, that it is biased towards the mainstream Hollywood film and that it leaves little room for deviation from a conventional linear mode of storytelling. Nevertheless, it does not prescribe substance or content – 'the paradigm is a form, not a formula; it's what holds the story together.' (p14)

These perceived limitations of Field's approach, however, could be seen as strengths when devising exercises for students, who will find some security in the inflexibility of the Three Act paradigm. Despite the reservations above, it does offer a reliable method of organising a story for the screen and ensuring that the requirements of a mainstream audience are kept in mind. A useful exercise is to identify Plot Points in a range of films in class and discuss in detail how narrative machinery operates.

The Three Act Structure is a useful basis for work on film narrative, even if, initially, some students argue that they are not interested in developing conventional fictions. As suggested previously, it is probably unwise to allow students to pursue more esoteric or abstract works before they understand the principles of conventional story telling. Some students will seek to avoid conventional modes of narration and insist that their ideas cannot be creatively constrained, but it is unlikely that their knowledge of convention is sufficiently sophisticated to challenge it successfully. Although we do not want simply to collude in the perpetuation of orthodox work, allowing students to side step narrative work can deprive them of the opportunity to demonstrate skills in the manipulation of film form.

• Christopher Vogler, *The Writer's Journey*

Starting life as a seven-page memo when the author was a story analyst at Disney, Vogler's book has acquired legendary status. Inspired by the mythologist Joseph Campbell's *The Hero with a Thousand Faces*, which Vogler describes as 'not an invention, but an observation ... a recognition of a beautiful design, a set of principles that govern the conduct of life and the world of storytelling the way physics and chemistry govern the physical world', *The Writer's Journey* emphasises the importance of mythic structure and mythic archetypes when constructing screenplays. With reference to Jungian and Freudian psychology it also attributes redemptive and restorative powers to the most popular stories to account for their appeal.

Vogler argues that great films are such because they 'have an appeal that can be felt by everyone, because they well up from a universal source in the shared unconscious and reflect universal concerns'. He schematises the universal pattern of 'The Hero's Journey' thus:

- Ordinary World
- Call to Adventure
- Refusal of the Call
- Meeting with the Mentor
- Crossing the First Threshold
- Tests, Allies, Enemies
- Approach to the Innermost Cave
- Ordeal
- Reward (Seizing the Sword)
- The Road Back
- Resurrection
- Return with the Elixir.

Vogler stresses that the elements of 'The Hero's Journey' are not necessarily literally realised in a screenplay (although this can be the case – in *Star Wars*, for example), but that they can be manifested in a variety of guises. Similarly, he argues that the most common archetypes (Hero, Mentor, Threshold Guardian, Herald, Shapeshifter, Shadow, Trickster) should not necessarily be seen as fixed characters, but as *functions* of the narrative which can be adopted by different characters at different times.

The thesis is demonstrated with reference to various films and put to the test in relation to *The Full Monty*:

- The 'Ordinary World' of Sheffield is established (in order to provide a contrast with the 'special world' which the men will enter).
- Gaz's 'Call to Adventure' occurs when he sees his ex-wife and her friends at the male strip show.
- The 'Refusal of the Call' comes from his friends with their doubts and insecurities.
- The 'Meeting with the Mentor' is represented by Horse – the best dancer, and Gerald – the professional who takes dancing lessons and also by Nathan (a 'wise young man').
- 'Crossing the First Threshold' is where Gaz holds auditions for the show which marks the men's transition into the new 'special world'.
- He also transforms an 'enemy' (Gerald) into an 'ally'.
- The 'Approach to the Innermost Cave' is the phase of preparation and rehearsal.
- The 'Ordeal' is when Dave wants to quit (tied up with his feelings of sexual inadequacy) and the men are arrested for indecent exposure.
- The 'Reward' which follows is the news that the arrest has been good publicity and Dave's reassurance from his wife that she loves him.
- 'The Road Back' features Dave's renewed enthusiasm and courage as he rejoins his friends in the final preparations for the act.

- On the night Gaz gets cold feet, his involvement 'dies', but he then undergoes 'Resurrection' when Nathan persuades him to go on.
- Gaz joins his friends in time to pass the final test of commitment and they reveal themselves totally – this is the 'Return with the Elixir' of co-operation, self-knowledge and self-respect.

This application of Vogler's thesis demonstrates how the paradigm is not wholly convincing in all circumstances. It's hard to see Horse/Gerald/Nathan as analogues of Obi Wan Kenobi, for example, although, arguably, they have a vaguely similar function at different points. But it does illustrate many functions which are common to different screen narratives.

It is less successful when mapping 'The Hero's Journey' onto the conventional Three Act Structure popularised by Syd Field, as this pins 'Crossing the First Threshold' to the start of Act II and 'The Road Back' to the start of Act III. In *The Full Monty* example, this would mean that the second act does not start until nearly halfway through the film and, indeed, the marriage of the two paradigms is undermined when Vogler writes:

> 'The structure should not call attention to itself, nor should it be followed too precisely. The order of the stages given here is only one of many possible variations. The stages can be deleted added to, and drastically shuffled without losing any of their power.' (p26)

In other examples Vogler demonstrates flexible, contingent applications of 'The Hero's Journey' and stresses that it should not be followed slavishly as a formula, but that writers should 'challenge these ideas, test them in practice, adapt them to your needs and … use these concepts to challenge and inspire your own stories.'

This is possibly the most useful application of *The Writer's Journey* – as a script editing tool. When discussing students' story ideas, for example, it can be illuminating to refer to some of the archetypes and mythic structures in Vogler's book in order to realise how a narrative hole can be plugged or peril be increased. If it is offered as a template it will produce predictable and possibly depressing results.

Screenplay basics

Understanding the nature of stories is fundamental to this work. We may seem to be experts when evaluating other people's stories, but creating our own from scratch presents more of a challenge. Enabling our students to become competent storytellers needs to be achieved through, initially, examining existing stories and establishing some principles which will be reinforced through subsequent exercises.

Screenplay format

Worksheet 1

This is a simple exercise to introduce students to the format and nomenclature of screenplays. It can be a very brief group activity and be used as a consolidation exercise.

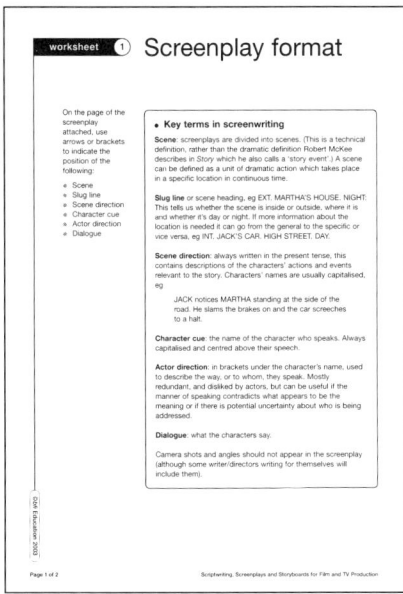

Worksheet 2

This exercise is, at one level, a simple 'translation' exercise – taking a story in one form and re-telling it in another. However, it also creates opportunities for different emphases, different points of view and different characters to emerge, all of which can be usefully analysed in a debriefing session.

In small groups students are given a short story or fable – the worksheet uses the urban legend *The Vanishing Hitchhiker*.

> A girl and her father were driving along a country road on their way home when they saw a young girl hitchhiking. They stopped and picked her up and she got in the back seat. She told the girl and her father that she lived in a house about five miles up the road. She didn't say anything after that but just turned to watch out the window. When the father saw the house he drove up to it and turned around to tell the girl they had arrived – but she wasn't there. Both he and his daughter were really mystified and decided to knock on the door and tell the people what had happened. They told him they had once had a daughter who answered the description of the girl they supposedly had picked up, but she had disappeared some years ago and had last been seen hitchhiking on this very road. Today would have been her birthday.

From this very short story, students are asked to construct a short screenplay, using the conventions outlined above. Preparatory discussion should encourage consideration of the following:

- How many scenes will it entail? (Everyone should realise that it will require at least two – inside the car and at the house of the strange girl's parents – but there may be some creative suggestions for more.)
- What is the road like? Why?
- What is the light like? Why?
- What do the characters look and sound like? Why?
- How do they act? What sorts of things do they do? How do we know what they are feeling?
- What do they say? Do they say what they mean?
- What is the house like? Why?
- What do the people who live there look like? How do they behave? What is their relationship like? How do we know?

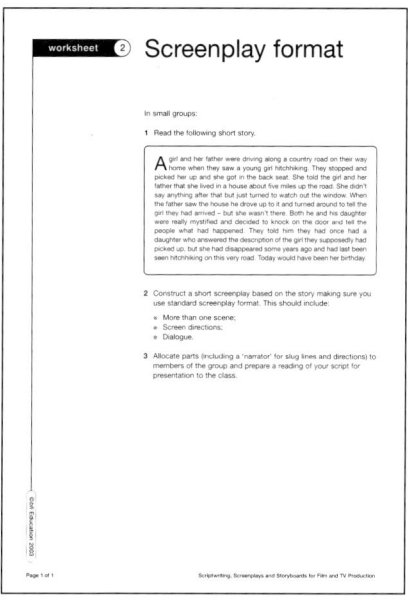

Our primary objectives here are to get students to practise writing in screenplay format and thinking visually. It is also an opportunity for them to practise writing dialogue and constructing characters. It is an early writing exercise and, therefore, offers the security of a pre-existing (very simple) story and collaboration.

The resulting scripts can be given dramatised readings by casting the different characters and using a 'narrator' for scene headings and screen directions. The success of each can then be assessed. Discussions should highlight some of the general issues and problems to be confronted when constructing screenplays – aspects of which will be addressed separately in later exercises.

Story structure

Worksheet 3

Short stories and fables provide excellent examples for analysis as they offer simplicity and manageability, yet can effectively illuminate key aspects of the machinery of storytelling. These stories can generate useful discussion about character, resolution, logical causality and theme.

● Activity 1

This exercise takes Aesop's fable, *The Slave and the Lion* (although an equivalent alternative would work just as well), in order to achieve an understanding of the following concepts:

- A story comprises a series of interconnected events which lead to a resolution (logical causality);
- Narrative functions and their uses;
- 'Goal-oriented protagonist';
- Theme or 'controlling idea'.

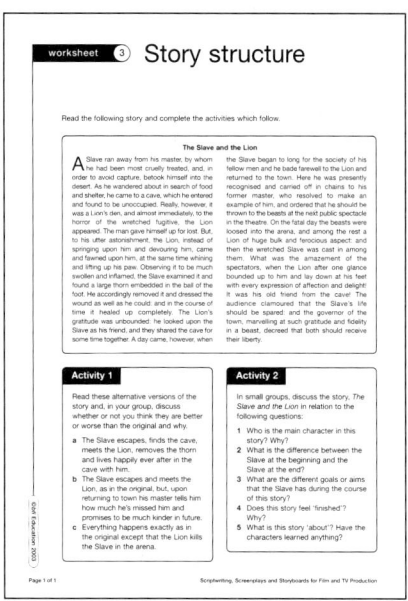

The Slave and the Lion

A Slave ran away from his master, by whom he had been most cruelly treated, and, in order to avoid capture, betook himself into the desert. As he wandered about in search of food and shelter, he came to a cave, which he entered and found to be unoccupied. Really, however, it was a Lion's den, and almost immediately, to the horror of the wretched fugitive, the Lion appeared. The man gave himself up for lost. But, to his utter astonishment, the Lion, instead of springing upon him and devouring him, came and fawned upon him, at the same time whining and lifting up his paw. Observing it to be much swollen and inflamed, the Slave examined it and found a large thorn embedded in the ball of the foot. He accordingly removed it and dressed the wound as well as he could: and in the course of time it healed up completely. The Lion's gratitude was unbounded: he looked upon the Slave as his friend, and they shared the cave for some time together. A day came, however, when the Slave began to long for the society of his fellow men and he bade farewell to the Lion and returned to the town. Here he was presently recognised and carried off in chains to his former master, who resolved to make an example of him, and ordered that he should be thrown to the beasts at the next public spectacle in the theatre. On the fatal day the beasts were loosed into the arena, and among the rest a Lion of huge bulk and ferocious aspect: and then the wretched Slave was cast in among them. What was the amazement of the spectators, when the Lion after one glance bounded up to him and lay down at his feet with every expression of affection and delight! It was his old friend from the cave! The audience clamoured that the Slave's life should be spared: and the governor of the town, marvelling at such gratitude and fidelity in a beast, decreed that both should receive their liberty.

Alternative versions

a) The Slave escapes, finds the cave, meets the Lion, removes the thorn and lives happily ever after in the cave with him.

b) The Slave escapes and meets the Lion, as in the original, but, upon returning to town his master tells him how much he's missed him and promises to be much kinder in future.

c) Everything happens exactly as in the original except that the Lion kills the Slave in the arena.

The substitutions and deletions can be excellent exercises to prime students for subsequent analytical work. The three alternative versions of the story and the questions about them should lead to some fruitful discussion about the nature of narrative and resolution.

This simple exercise should produce immediate focus on specific elements of the story which generate interest and create empathy, tension and surprise elements which, in short, make it a story rather than a sequence of random events with no sense of resolution. Alternative version (a) produces a 'so what?' effect – it's possible that there could be a story about a man living with a lion, but there is nothing here to develop that. It also deprives us of a confrontation between the Slave and his master and enables us to realise that this story revolves around that particular conflict. Version (b) offers us more information, more events, but there is no causal connection between the Slave's good deed for the Lion and his subsequent better treatment by his master, so what's the point of it? In addition, it reveals how the original version creates more jeopardy and sustains tension. Version (c) reads a bit like a joke, but even as a comic reversal of expectations it's unsatisfying because, surely, the Lion is acting 'out of character' – his previous relationship with the slave makes this action unmotivated and implausible.

Despite its simplicity, this exercise should produce some valuable responses and insights which should be articulated and recorded; lack of character motivation, randomness of events and lack of narrative development are all common problems with students' work and this can be a useful reference point in the future.

● Activity 2

Following Activity 1, students could work in small groups in order to consider questions which focus on the nature of the main character in the story, the way in which the story is built around his 'journey' and the significant moments in the story which cause other things to happen. Subsequent discussion could evolve along the following lines:

1 The Slave is the main character because:

- We see things from his point of view and, therefore, identify most with him;
- He is 'on screen' most of the time;
- He initiates the action and drives the plot;
- The story describes his journey.

These points together can usefully define the term **protagonist** (the terms 'hero' or 'heroine' are often used instead, but students may assume that a 'hero' must be 'heroic'. The term 'protagonist' sidesteps this issue.)

2 At the beginning the Slave is a fugitive on the run. At the end he is a legitimately free man. He has travelled a path and achieved his ultimate goal as a direct result of his actions.

3 The Slave's goals vary.
- Initially he wants to escape from his cruel master.
- In the cave he wants to survive his encounter with the Lion.

- Then he wants to help the lion.
- Later he wants to return to human company.
- Subsequently he wants to survive his ordeal in the arena.

There is an opportunity here to highlight those moments at which a goal changes or is reached and nominate them as turning points, reversals, or **Plot Points**.

4 The story feels finished because the protagonist has attained his ultimate goal. That goal has been achieved as a direct result of his actions. Although the Slave's fictional 'life' could continue, our interest in it ceases at the point at which he wins his freedom.

5 The question of theme or controlling idea can generate some useful discussion. It clearly operates around the poles of 'cruelty' and 'kindness' and also 'humanity' and 'beastliness'. The slave has been treated cruelly and runs away. Later, despite being fearful, he is kind to a beast. Upon his return, humans consign him to a cruel fate, but the beast repays his kindness with kindness of its own. Finally, marvelling at this display of 'humanity', the governor rewards both beast and man with freedom – in other words the beast teaches men how to be kind. Even if a formulation such as 'kindness will be repaid' seems a bit reductive, it should be clear that there is a high degree of thematic unity in this story which holds the action together and which conveys a moral message.

It can also be suggested that this unity and sense of balance deters us from questioning the coincidence upon which the resolution depends – it is clearly a contrivance which serves the story, but our pleasure in seeing the different strands come together in order to bring about the resolution makes it unlikely that we will question the 'reality' of the tale. Once again, this can be a useful reference point later when students attempt to pin their own work to some kind of controlling idea.

Worksheet 4 – Analysing *Friends*

A predictive exercise can help to develop and extend what has been learned in relation to the fable. Again, an example has been chosen which is short enough to be manageable in its entirety. It is also a very different kind of text, which has two advantages: it introduces variety and it also demonstrates that structural similarities can be identified in different forms from different periods.

The example below is from *Friends* (Season 2, Episode 21 – 'The one with the bullies'). Like many recent US sitcoms it exemplifies a highly condensed economical mode of story telling; in 22 minutes of screen time this episode contains three distinct stories, each of which reaches a resolution. Each story is told in five or six scenes and, as there is no room for superfluous narrative material, they provide excellent material for investigating story construction and causality.

For ease of reference, the following breakdown of the episode includes only the essential bits of narrative information and each element is preceded by an A, B or C, depending on which story it relates to (no hierarchy of stories should be inferred from this).

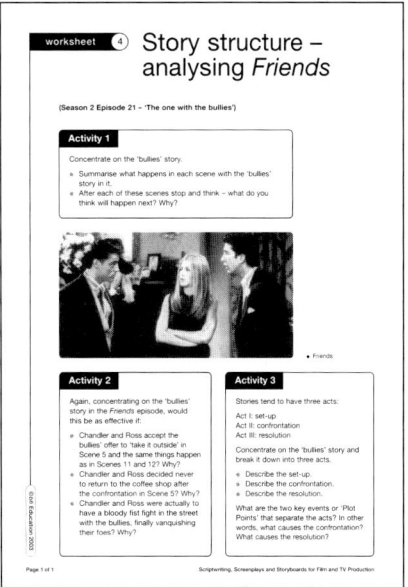

Scene 1 (teaser)

B   Monica is unemployed and short of money. She's been watching the business channel and has noticed that there is some stock which corresponds to her initials.

C   Phoebe decides to visit her estranged father because she has been interpreting a range of everyday occurrences as 'signs' which are telling her to go.

Scene 2

A   Ross and Chandler are moved from their usual seat in the coffee house, Central Perk, by two intimidating men who claim to have been sitting there before them. One of them takes Chandler's hat and refuses to return it.

Scene 3

B   Monica has had an interview for a terrible job at a fifties themed restaurant. She can't bear to think about taking it but she is desperately short of money and may have to.

A   Chandler and Ross return and describe how they were bullied.

B   Monica notices that the stock with her initials has gone up and suddenly decides to play the market.

Scene 4

C   Phoebe arrives at her father's house with Joey and Rachel, but is chased away by an aggressive dog.

Scene 5

A   Ross and Chandler meet the bullies again in Central Perk. The bullies claim ownership of the sofa and, after some verbal sparring, suggest that they take their dispute 'outside'. Chandler and Ross back down and the bullies tell them never to return to the coffee shop.

Scene 6

C   Night has fallen and the dog has disappeared, but Phoebe thinks that the dog was a 'bad sign' and that perhaps the meeting is not meant to be after all. She drives away and accidentally runs over the dog.

ADVERT BREAK

Scene 7

B   Monica has been transformed into an enthusiastic trader and is confidently buying shares over the phone.

C   Phoebe reveals that the dog is at the vet's and will be OK. She feels obliged to let the dog's owner know, but doesn't want her first contact with her father to be over the phone and about his damaged dog. Joey phones for her and explains that the dog will be returned shortly.

Scene 8

A   Chandler and Ross drink instant cappuccino in Chandler's apartment, putting a brave face on their enforced exile from Central Perk. Joey offers to escort them later, but Ross becomes infuriated by the situation and argues that they should stand up to the bullies.

Scene 9

B   Monica is desperate – she has lost all her money and wants to borrow money from Rachel or she'll have to take the job in the diner. Rachel can't help her.

Scene 10

C   Phoebe returns the dog to her father's house. She discovers that her father left four years ago, but meets her half brother Frank with whom she establishes some kind of rapport.

Scene 11

A   Ross and Chandler 'bravely' gulp down their coffee in Central Perk and, having asserted their right to be there, dash out. However, they meet the bullies outside. They all prepare to fight, and, after outlawing them as potential weapons, put their keys and watches in a hat. They take some time to establish rules of engagement and, meanwhile, their stuff is stolen by a couple of opportunist thieves.

Scene 12

A   Ross and Chandler return to the coffee house with the bullies, flushed with success at their triumph over the thieves. They have all bonded through the experience and decide that they no longer have a problem with each other.

Scene 13 (Tag)

B   Monica is suffering at her new job in the fifties diner.

This scene breakdown is available as a student handout at www.bfi.org.uk/tfms.

● **Activity 1**

Our objectives with this exercise are to achieve understanding of:

● Causality
● The nature of resolution
● The nature of 'acts'.

A useful way in is to pick one of the stories, let's say, 'the bullies' and:

● Prime students to focus on that story alone;
● Play the episode and, after each scene which builds that story, pause and ask for predictions about how it will develop.

This tight focus on a single strand of the episode can be extremely productive as it makes it harder for students to be distracted by the many other (amusing and entertaining) elements. It also enables a rigorous focus to be maintained on narrative issues rather than comedic ones. In fact, it should become apparent that there is nothing inherently comedic about any of the stories and that the comedy is generated through the treatment of the situations, the reactions of the characters and the dialogue.

Even early discussions about the story are likely to elicit suggestions that, somehow, by the end Ross and Chandler will have managed to solve the problem of the bullies without having to undergo any major changes themselves; there will already be awareness (which may need to be reformulated) that it is a convention of this particular genre, the situation comedy, that the status quo is restored by the end of the episode.

● **Activity 2**

As with the fable, it is worth introducing alternative narrative elements in order to generate an understanding of why this story 'works' in this form. Suggest the following:

- What if Chandler and Ross accept the bullies' offer to 'take it outside' in Scene 5 and the same things happen as in Scenes 11 and 12? Does this work as well? No, because we would have leaped from the establishment of the problem to the resolution of the problem, with no development.
- What if, for example, Chandler and Ross decided never to return to the coffee shop after the confrontation in Scene 5 – would this be a satisfying story? No, because it deprives us of a resolution to the problem. We would keenly feel the need for a further confrontation leading to a resolution.
- If Chandler and Ross were actually to have a bloody fist fight in the street with the bullies, finally vanquishing their foes, would this feel like a satisfying resolution? Probably not, as this would not conform to the type of resolution which the genre demands.

• Activity 3

This exercise should make it clear that, even though it is common to read about the 'Two Act Structure' of situation comedy (especially in a commercial TV context where an ad break separates the two parts), we actually have three acts here, albeit in a highly condensed form:

- Act I can be seen as the establishment of the problem – there are 'bullies' in Central Perk who have taken against Ross and Chandler.
- Act II is the development and elaboration of this problem which begins with the second confrontation and includes the threat, the misery of exile, the decision to stand up to the enemy and the 'last stand' in the coffee house.
- Act III, the resolution, begins when Ross and Chandler bump into the bullies – there is no return from this moment. Although initially it seems as if the resolution will be effected through violence, this is neatly avoided through the sudden introduction of a common enemy against whom they unite and afterwards settle their differences.

This example should emphasise the importance of seeing acts as dramatic movements, rather than mechanical junctions (the act breaks in Phoebe's and Monica's respective stories obviously occur at different points in the episode). It can also be made clear that these movements are dependent upon, as Phil Parker suggests '[the audience's] engagement with the narrative as a whole… and the development of individual characters' stories and thematic concerns' (p27), so this story can really be seen to be about Ross and Chandler overcoming their innate desire to avoid conflict (significantly Joey is repeatedly deterred from getting involved). Consequently the elaboration in Act II centres upon the escalation of their unhappiness until it reaches such a point that, despite their lack of fighting skills, they decide to confront the enemy.

Worksheet 5

A game of 'consequences' can provide a light-hearted interlude or a close to a session, while actually performing a valuable function – it necessitates logical sequencing of narrative events.

The idea is simple – students are offered a narrative 'set up' and then take it in turns to suggest a narrative event which logically follows on and which builds the story, leading to a resolution.

This is a very flexible format – it can be used with a whole group so that the responses are public, or it can be used to get small groups of students to create a story and then provide

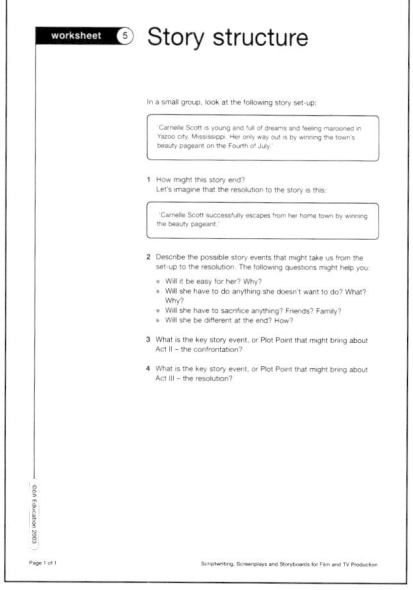

feedback to the group. If it is used as a whole group exercise, requiring fast thinking and responding, it may be useful to impose some rules, for example:

- Each student may introduce only one new character;
- Anyone may 'buzz' and veto a suggestion if they believe it does not follow logically, or have the potential to advance the story;
- If the original suggestion is defended to the satisfaction of the majority, the challenger forfeits a turn.

The results of the activity in this format may not always constitute an entirely coherent narrative, but the game does provoke critical thinking about the nature of stories, can stimulate useful debate about the nature of narrative and should be fun. If necessary the 'chair' can suggest that someone needs to throw in a surprise or turning point or that the students need to move towards a resolution. Upon reaching the end, a debrief can reveal and illuminate the ways in which particular aspects of the collectively told story worked or not. Starting points can be invented, or found, for example, in film blurbs in the *Radio Times*. Here are some examples that would make useful beginnings:

- 'On receiving a hobby horse as a Christmas present, young Paul Grahame discovers a strange gift for guessing the winners of real horse races.'
- 'Carnelle Scott is young and full of dreams and feeling marooned in Yazoo city, Mississippi. Her only way out is by winning the town's beauty pageant on the Fourth of July.'

- 'A lonely teacher strikes up a correspondence with a prison inmate. When the convict is released he heads for his penpal's door, anxious to reveal a startling secret.'
- 'Stanton Carlisle is intrigued by a mind-reading act at a carnival, but his ambition leads to tragedy.'
- 'Three people living in 'Small Town', Minnesota, discover a crashed plane that contains a dead pilot and over $4 million in cash. They decide to steal the money, but their plan soon begins to backfire.'

An additional strategy, which offers a bit more security of outcome, is for the group to decide on a possible resolution to the story before embarking on the steps towards it. The 'closed' version and the 'open' version can be implemented as written exercises if it is more appropriate and, perhaps used as the basis for brainstorming activities in the initial stages of a project. Worksheet 5 takes the second example and treats it as a written exercise, suggesting a resolution to the story.

All of these simple questions are designed to generate focus on character and conflict and should ensure that the narrative suggestions are based on a higher degree of shared knowledge.

Case Study: *Joyride* (Jim Gillespie, 1995, UK)

See www.bfi.org.uk/tfms for details of ordering this film.

There are some obvious advantages to using a film such as this:

- It is short (10 minutes) and, therefore, a whole group viewing and re-viewing can easily be accommodated in class time.
- It has a self-contained narrative structure which makes it possible to analyse beginnings, endings and Plot Points.
- Its production values are quite high so it feels like a 'proper' film which could be (and, in fact was) screened theatrically.

Many short films can work equally well in this context, although if one of the goals is to examine logical causality, it may be best to avoid some of the more abstract examples. FilmFour regularly includes shorts in its schedule; Channel 4's 'Shooting Gallery' strand is a good source for short films; and the BBC still shows '10x10' films and 'Tartan Shorts' occasionally.

● Synopsis

The film opens at night, there are sounds of a storm brewing in the distance. An engineer is on the phone to a colleague as he inspects a faulty overhead power line. He tells his colleague that the fault is not serious and that he is late for a date so he packs up and leaves.

Changing his shirt while driving, he stops abruptly when he notices a body in the road. He gets out, approaches the body but, when the 'body' turns to look at him and another man approaches him from behind, he realises that this is a set-up. The second man knocks him out.

He wakes up, hands tied, in the boot of his own car, which is now being driven by his attackers. He manages to switch on a torch and then kicks at one of the rear light clusters, in order to disconnect the wiring. The car is then noticed by two police officers who give chase. The ambushers pull over and field questions about the rear light, but when the kidnapped engineer kicks and shouts from inside the boot, and is heard by the police, the villains attack and, we assume, kill them.

The journey resumes and the engineer frantically tries to cut his bonds with a knife from his tool kit. Another police car is now in pursuit and, as it bumps the pursued car, it causes the loose wiring on the light to spark and for a can of petrol to spill over the engineer. With his hands free, the engineer pulls out the main fuse, cutting the power to lights and engine and the car veers off the road, into some woods and crashes.

He staggers from the wreckage – one of the attackers has gone through the windscreen – and makes for the road where the police car has stopped, but the other attacker seizes him from behind and holds a knife to his throat to ensure his silence. Suddenly one of the loose wires from the fuse box makes contact again and the car alarm goes off, alerting the police to their presence. Threatening to kill his hostage, the attacker demands the police car and the police agree and back off, but the engineer, drawing on his last reserves of energy, lunges backwards and knocks down his tormentor.

A policeman helps the engineer out of the woods and comments on the smell of petrol. The engineer realises that he has ended up where he started, at the site of the faulty power line. He calls out to the policeman that, if he had fixed the fault, he would never have met his attackers. As he looks up there is a crackle and a shower of sparks and we cut to black with the sound of sudden combustion.

This synopsis is available as a student handout at www.bfi.org.uk/tfms.

Story structure and theme

Worksheet 6

● Activity 1 – Story structure

Joyride provides opportunities to illuminate significant elements in film narratives through some quite simple exercises. It should be possible, subsequently, for students to engage in discussions about the validity of the causality and theme in their own work in an informed way. Students should describe the causal connections between the events, creating a set of sentences using the word 'because'. This is a useful exercise as it should provide them with a reference point when planning the

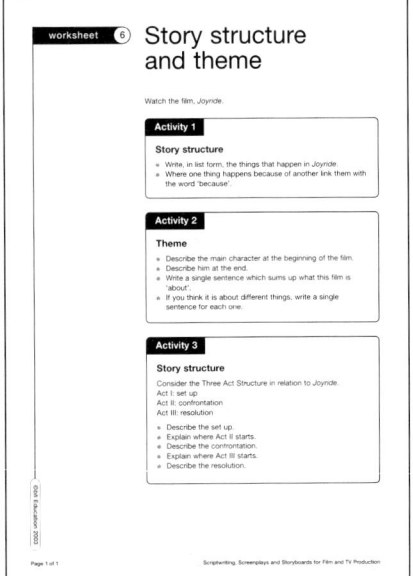

sequence of events in their own work and may ensure that they avoid causality gaps. The exercise creates an opportunity for students to discuss the events in the film and the causal links between them.

A feedback session, in which the results are written on the board or OHP may produce something like this:

1 Because the engineer puts off fixing the fault he arrives at the ambush point at just the 'right' time;
2 Because he thinks someone is injured he gets out of the car to have a look;
3 Because he kicks out the rear light the police stop the car;
4 Because he shouts from inside the boot the attackers kill the police officers;
5 Because the police car bumps the back of the pursued car the petrol spills on the engineer;
6 Because he has kicked out the light there are sparks flying from the wires;
7 Because he disconnects the fuse the car goes out of control;
8 Because the engineer has a knife at his throat he can't call out to the police;
9 Because the fuse wire briefly makes a connection the alarm goes off;
10 Because the alarm goes off the police are able to locate the attacker;
11 Because the attacker is distracted the engineer is able to overcome him;
12 Because he has not fixed the power line it is still sparking;
13 Because he is soaked in petrol he catches fire when he is showered with sparks.

There is an opportunity here to use the film as an illustration of Robert McKee's definition of causality:

> 'Causality drives a story in which motivated actions cause effects that in turn become the causes of yet other effects, thereby interlinking the various levels of conflict in a chain reaction of episodes to the Story Climax.' (*Story*, p52)

The above list is a very neat one, but subjecting the film's sequence of events to closer scrutiny may encourage some students to argue that there are some causal gaps in the film. How, for example, does a second police car appear so quickly? How exactly does the engineer manage to overcome his assailant? Isn't it rather unlikely that the fuse wire should connect in such way as to set off the alarm at just the moment it is needed? How plausible is it that the engineer should find himself back where he started? This opens up a debate about whether the film provides us with sufficient evidence to suspend our disbelief. When we see the police officers, for example, we hear the radio crackling in the background and, therefore, it is possible that they could have called for back up.

The engineer's sudden overthrow of his attacker is a little trickier to rationalise, especially as the move he makes is unclear – a reverse headbutt? Nevertheless, the alarm and the arrival of the police provide grounds for arguing that villain is distracted and off his guard. The unexpected electrical connection may open up a debate around the role of electricity in the film as a whole and may elicit the idea that the image of electrical sparks is a motif in this piece. It could be argued, therefore, that the film coherently constructs electricity as an unpredictable, elemental force and that, therefore, the sudden fortuitous connection is 'in character'. (This could be examined in relation to the 'Controlling Idea' in the next section.) The key point here is to identify logical cause and effect and to decide whether or not the events in the film are sufficiently motivated to allow us to suspend our disbelief.

● **Activity 2 – Theme**

Robert McKee chooses the term 'Controlling Idea' over theme and explains

> 'a Controlling Idea may be expressed in a single sentence describing how and why life undergoes change from one condition of existence at the beginning to another at the end.' (*Story*, p115)

Examination of this is a natural progression from looking at causality. Some fruitful discussion could be generated from posing the simple question 'what is this film about'? It may be that there are a number of answers to this question, but it is important that each is weighed up against the available evidence.

The first task is to identify what McKee calls the 'value in its positive or negative charge that comes into the world or life of [a] character as a result of the final action of the story'.

Another task, then, is for students to:

● Describe the main character at the beginning of the film;
● Describe him at the end.

The descriptions of his state at the beginning, such as cheerful, confident, careless, anticipating sex (he is 'on a promise'), should contrast with descriptions of his state at the end, such as battered, fearful, wounded, and possibly dead.

Having established the change in 'value' from positive to negative, the next step is to attribute the main cause to that change. A leading question might be: 'Does the engineer deserve what happens to him?', which should produce responses that address the negligence of the protagonist as well as his unluckiness.

This provides a good foundation for the next step which asks students in small groups to write a sentence which sums up what this film is 'about', or more than one if they think it is about different things. An example can be offered, perhaps a flippant one just to kick-start the activity, such as:

'Don't drive in the rain or you'll get ambushed.'

A feedback session will hopefully elicit such suggestions as:

● 'Don't put things off or you might pay a price for it.'
● 'There is no place for a good Samaritan – the world is a cruel place.'
● 'Don't betray your professional responsibilities.'
● 'Don't be complacent – you might get surprised by something unpleasant.'

The justification for any one of these positions will require specific reference to the causal relationships in the film and the nature of the protagonist and the way in which he engages with his world. This work provides a useful reference point when discussing the Controlling Idea of more complex film narratives and when discussing with students the Controlling Idea which determines their own story design.

● Activity 3 – Story structure

There is also an opportunity to illuminate the notion of the Three Act Structure in relation to this film – students could be assigned the task of identifying the Plot Points as described in Syd Field's paradigm (*Screenplay*, p9). This may seem like an artificial exercise, given the length of the film, but, despite its brevity, it is possible to discern three distinct segments in the film and to identify the moments at which the story is spun in a different direction. This exercise could be carried out, like the others, in a discursive context, or it could be an individual, paper-based exercise, in which students are asked to break down the film into its dramatic acts.

It should be clear to students that:

● Act I establishes the situation, the main character and his goal (to make his 'date'). The Plot Point which changes this is the discovery of the 'body' in the middle of the road and his subsequent capture.
● Act II begins with the protagonist trapped in his own car boot. His 'confrontation' with his assailants comprises attempts to draw attention to his plight and escape, each of which puts him in more peril, culminating in the desperate action which sends the car out of control.
● Act III begins as the protagonist gets out of the boot (his Act II goal achieved) but suddenly the stakes change and he becomes a hostage with a knife at his throat. He overcomes this last obstacle and the authorities move in to restore order, but there is a sting in the tail as he is 'hoist with his own petard'.

Again, this can make a useful reference point when students are planning their own work. Given that they are likely to be producing a script or video extract, rather than complete work, it is useful to choose a key moment or a turning point in the story. An understanding of screenplay design and terminology can help students to plan story events which are meaningful within and supported by a wider context.

Story types and genres

Work on story types can easily be linked with work on genres and focuses less on story structure and more on the nature of particular types of set-ups, confrontations and resolutions.

Worksheet 7 – Story types

The following taxonomy can be used as a basis for approaching any narrative and can help students to determine (in both their own and other people's work) where the main story lies, what the subsidiary stories are and who the protagonists are.

Developing the notion of eight essential plots ('Achilles', 'Candide', 'Cinderella', 'Circe', 'Faust', 'Orpheus', 'Romeo and Juliet' and 'Tristan') Phil Parker suggests that there are in fact ten basic stories which are commonly found in screen narratives (*The Art and Science of Screenwriting* pp77–79) and lists them thus (his explanations have been paraphrased):

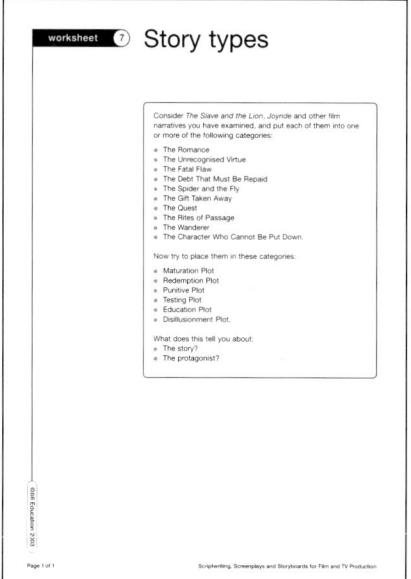

1   The Romance

A character is seen to be emotionally lacking or missing something or someone. Something/someone – the object of desire – is seen as a potential solution. The character struggles to overcome barriers between himself and the object of desire and succeeds in overcoming some, if not all, of them. The resolution comes when the character unites with the object of desire (eg *When Harry Met Sally,* Rob Reiner, 1989, US).

2   The Unrecognised Virtue

The character with a virtue becomes part of someone else's world and falls in love with a powerful character in this world. The character seeks to prove that she is desirable to the powerful character but the power relationship undermines this. The character attempts to solve a problem for the powerful character and, in doing so, her virtue is finally recognised (eg *Pretty Woman*, Garry Marshall, US, 1990).

3   The Fatal Flaw

The character has a quality that brings success and enables him to gain opportunities denied to other characters. He uses opportunities for his own gain at the expense of others, but when he recognises the damage he has done he sets himmself a new challenge. However, the quality which brought him success leads to failure in the new challenge (eg William Shakespeare's *Macbeth*).

4 The Debt That Must Be Repaid

The character wants something or someone and becomes aware that something or someone is available which will possibly give her what she wants – at a price. The character agrees to pay the price later and pursues her original desire. The character attempts to avoid settling the debt but is finally confronted by the debtor and the debt is repaid (eg *Dr Jekyll and Mr Hyde* by Robert Louis Stevenson).

5 The Spider and the Fly

The character wants to make another character do his bidding but, having no power to force her, devises a plan to trap her into doing it. The character successfully executes the plan, achieves his initial goal and then faces a new future (eg *Double Indemnity*, Billy Wilder, US, 1944).

6 The Gift Taken Away

The character has a gift which she loses and seeks to regain. The pursuit of the gift leads her into a new situation to which she becomes reconciled (eg *Rain Man*, Barry Levinson, US, 1988).

7 The Quest

The character is set a task to find someone or something. He accepts the challenge, searches for and finds the someone or something. He is then rewarded, or not, for his success in the quest (eg *Star Wars*, George Lucas, US, 1977).

8 The Rites of Passage

The character recognises that she has reached the next 'age' in her life and attempts to learn what she needs to know to adapt to this new age. She tries to act as if she has already acquired the necessary knowledge and fails. She then encounters a challenge which requires her to reach beyond what she has already achieved. Her success reflects her maturation into the new phase of her life (eg *Stand by Me*, Rob Reiner, US, 1986).

9 The Wanderer

The character arrives in a new place and discovers a problem associated with it. In facing the problem she reveals why she left the last place, then attempts to move on again (eg *Shane*, George Stevens, US, 1953).

10 The Character Who Cannot Be Put Down

The character demonstrates his prowess in a certain situation but then faces a bigger challenge, which he accepts. He succeeds by triumphing over a range of antagonistic forces (eg *Die Hard,* John McTiernan, US, 1988).

In addition to this we have Christopher Vogler's master paradigm – 'The Hero's Journey' (outlined in Unit 1). In fact it's possible to argue that all of the above are simply specifically inflected versions of 'The Hero's Journey', especially give the predominance of references to 'challenges' and 'overcoming obstacles'.

Robert McKee also offers us a list of story types, a 'genre and sub-genre system used by screenwriters' (*Story,* pp80–81) which includes entries based on setting as well as story structure – the most useful of which are:

● Maturation Plot (the coming of age story);
● Redemption Plot (moral change in protagonist from bad to good);
● Punitive Plot (protagonist changes from good to bad and is punished);
● Testing Plot (willpower versus the temptation to surrender);
● Education Plot (protagonist's view of life/self/people changes from negative to positive);
● Disillusionment Plot (protagonist's worldview changes from positive to negative).

These notes on story types and plot types are available as a student handout at www.bfi.org.uk/tfms.

The six plots extracted from McKee's longer list have the advantage of being focused on story at the level of the protagonist's inner conflict and do not depend upon specific sets of actions. However, Parker stresses that the ten story types he offers 'are very basic and they can be used in numerous ways and combined in any grouping within any one narrative'. (p80)

No single definition, then, can hope to provide a wholly satisfactory account of a particular screen-work, but these taxonomies can provide some useful investigative starting points. Students can be asked to apply these models to any of the screen stories which are examined and should find that, for example, the 'spine' of a story, the motivation of the protagonist and the nature of the resolution all become clearer. If we take an example already discussed, *Joyride*, the apparent randomness of the encounter and the bleakness of the resolution might make more sense if one argues that it fits 'The Debt That Must Be Re-Paid' category. Similarly, a film such as *Groundhog Day*, discussed later, is illuminated if we approach it as an 'Education Plot' (or even 'Redemption Plot').

In addition to their usefulness as analytical approaches, these models can help students design their own screen stories by offering them possible routes through often confusing terrain: they may have a sense of the kinds of things they want to happen, but little sense of a coherent structure or development of the protagonist's character.

Case Study: *Groundhog Day* (Harold Ramis, 1993, US)

A typical assignment is likely to be an extract, rather than a full-length screenplay. Nevertheless, if our students have a sense of how a complete screenplay is structured they can make informed decisions about what sort of extract might be most interesting. They will also be able to discuss it in the context of the putative film from which it comes, understanding that every sequence has a specific role and has specific qualities.

Having examined a number of short examples it is necessary to consider at least one full length film, in order to establish its architecture in terms of Acts and Plot Points. *Groundhog Day* has been chosen here because, despite its appearance of simply replaying the same events over and over, it creates some excellent opportunities to discuss story progression, act structure, theme and character arc. Phil Parker describes its structure as 'circular', but unlike, say, *Pulp Fiction* (Quentin Tarantino, US, 1994), *About Adam* (Gerard Stembridge, UK, 2000) or *Lawless Heart* (Neil Hunter and Tom Hunsinger, UK/US, 2001), we do not simply witness the same events from different perspectives. Instead we have a strong sense of linear progression through the character of Phil Connors who stands outside of these repetitions and brings about change, at first exterior, but ultimately interior.

Synopsis

Cynical, egocentric Pittsburgh weatherman, Phil Connors, after making a 'no blizzard' prediction for the region, reluctantly journeys to Punxsutawney with his new producer, Rita, and cameraman, Larry in order to cover the annual Groundhog Day festivities (a ritual has developed around the idea that if the groundhog sees its shadow on February 2nd, there will supposedly be six more weeks of winter). They spend the night in Punxsutawney, cover the festival and head home, but are forced back by the blizzard Phil failed to anticipate.

Phil awakes next morning in his guest house and gradually realises that it is still February 2nd and that the day is repeating itself. Initially he thinks that he is ill but soon becomes intoxicated with the idea that, as the day starts afresh every morning, there are no consequences to his actions, and he exploits this by, for example, eating excessively, seducing a local woman and robbing a security van.

He then turns his attentions to Rita, using his special circumstances to discover her tastes and desires and fuel a calculated campaign of seduction. Despite repeated attempts to create the illusion that he is her ideal partner she continues to see through him and rejects him.

Phil then enters a state of despair and, after kidnapping the groundhog and driving over the edge of a quarry with it, repeatedly ends his life in a variety of ways, only to re-awaken every morning back in the guest house. Finally he unburdens himself to Rita, proving through his intimate knowledge of the local people and the events of the day that he is in an extraordinary state. She agrees to spend the rest of the day with him in order to see what happens but, later, they fall asleep in his room and when he wakes up he is alone again and it is February 2nd.

He then begins to live differently, treating people with respect and generosity, taking piano lessons and learning how to ice sculpt. He takes a particular interest in a tramp who, despite his best efforts, repeatedly dies. At the end of 'the day' he meets Rita at the party and she witnesses his musical prowess as well as the gratitude of the many people he has helped during the day. When the 'bachelor auction' commences she outbids everyone else for him and, after a walk during which Phil sculpts her face in ice and tells her he loves her, they spend a chaste night together.

The next morning Phil awakes to the same song that has played every morning, but quickly realises that Rita is still with him and that, at last, it is February 3rd and the 'spell' is broken.

This synopsis is available as a student handout at www.bfi.org.uk/tfms.

Story structure and types

Worksheet 8

• Activity 1 – structural analysis

A useful exercise is to examine how this film works in three acts, not simply to see how it fits some arbitrary paradigm, but to assess the effectiveness of the model. Does it have symmetry? Does it keep our interest engaged with regular 'bursts of energy'? Does it organise itself around logical narrative turning points, for example?

Syd Field insists that, before beginning to write a screenplay, the writer must know

- The ending
- Plot Point I
- Plot Point II

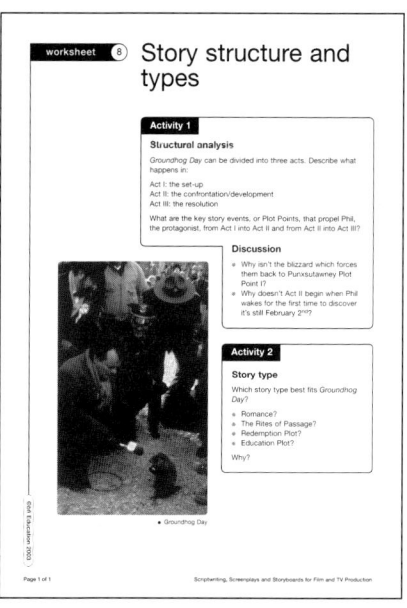

The two major Plot Points are the events which spin the action round into Act II and Act III respectively. However, it is probably a more straightforward task for students to attempt to identify the acts first – those units of dramatic action in which the protagonist has a clearly defined, specific goal which is differentiated from the others. Although Field's model is quite rigid and is based on the idea of the 120 page/120 minute screenplay, it is worth bearing in mind that the first act usually takes up about a quarter of the total time, the second act, half, and the final act, a quarter. In the case of *Groundhog Day*, which lasts about 95 minutes, we should be looking for act breaks at roughly 24 minutes and 71 minutes respectively. The results of such analysis might look like this:

Act I (Set-up):
The main characters are established through their actions: we learn that Phil is cynical about his work, egotistical and disparaging about his colleagues and the Punxsutawney festivities. Rita, in contrast, is genuine, innocent and full of enthusiasm for the report they are about to file on the groundhog celebrations. A look from Phil at Rita, his first sight of her, is the 'hook' – it suggests that his desire for her will drive the narrative (other 'Romantic Comedy' generic signifiers reinforce this interpretation). In Punxsutawney he is superior with the locals, delivers his report sarcastically and can't wait to get away, but is thwarted by the weather.

Plot Point I (@ 17 min):
Phil wakes up to discover it's still Groundhog Day. He spends the day bewildered and breaks a pencil before going to sleep.

Act II (Confrontation/Development) (@ 24 min):
Waking to find that the pencil is reconstituted, Phil now knows that this situation is something he must confront and try to solve. He sees a doctor, a psychiatrist and ends up in a bowling alley where a conversation with a couple of locals makes him realise that there are no consequences to his actions. The act proceeds through reckless abandonment (which includes the seduction of local woman Nancy), calculated pursuit of Rita, rejection, despair and attempted suicide. He then recruits Rita as an ally, leading to:

Plot Point II (@ 68 min):
In his guesthouse room, Phil tells Rita that the worst part of the situation is that 'tomorrow you'll have forgotten about this and think I'm a jerk again'. She says that maybe it's 'not a curse'.

Act III (Resolution) (@ 71 min):
A new dawn, literally and metaphorically. As a result of the insight expressed above, Phil embarks on a campaign of kindness, generosity and self improvement, culminating in the party and the walk back to the guest house, through which he earns Rita's love and frees himself from the trap of the repeating day.

Follow-up discussion

Despite the appearance of repetition, *Groundhog Day* has a great deal of forward momentum which is driven by 'the education of Phil Connors'. This is a film with a single protagonist whose arc or trajectory describes his movement from cynical and self-serving to selfless and loving. Consequently the Plot Points and act breaks are dependent upon his emotional development. Anticipating some debate about the location of the first plot point and start of Act II, it's worth addressing some questions:

● Why isn't the blizzard which forces them back to Punxsutawney Plot Point I?

There is a case for this, after all it effects a return to the town and conforms to the device of being 'sent back'. However, in itself, and in the context of the film, it is an irritant rather than an inciting incident; the weather could pass and Phil could return to Pittsburgh the next day if this were the only problem. Perhaps if the film was a 'natural disaster movie' the blizzard would then have greater significance, but in this context it does not propel Phil on his path towards change.

● Why doesn't Act II begin when Phil wakes for the first time to discover it's still February 2nd?

One could argue that this is where Phil's problems begin and that from this point on he tries to deal with them. However, his reaction at this point is bewilderment rather than purposefulness – he does not embark on a specific course of action to resolve the problem until he wakes up on the second morning and discovers that the pencil has been restored. Consequently, the second morning should be seen as Plot Point II (also known as a 'Turning Point' or 'Inciting Incident'), which, as Raymond Frensham argues, 'grabs the story, turns it around and catapults it in a new direction … raises the stakes of the story…increases momentum by raising the stakes … dramatically alters your protagonist's motivation'. (*Teach Yourself Screenwriting*, p108)

This last point is an important one and raises the question that, if the Acts – the 'movements' of the screenplay – are dependent upon the dramatic need of the protagonist, couldn't we argue that *Groundhog Day* has five acts, given the three distinct movements in the central act? It's true that in Act II Phil seems to have three different goals:

1 to have fun and treat Punxsutawney as his personal playground;
2 to seduce Rita; and
3 to end it all;

but, equally, these all come under the umbrella heading of 'development'. In addition, they are all negative, selfish goals. In contrast, after his day with Rita, at the end of which he displays self-knowledge for the first time (describing himself as a 'jerk' and telling her 'I don't deserve someone like you'), Act III commences with Phil's brand new agenda – to be generous and kind.

Activity 2 – Story type

In generic terms, *Groundhog Day* offers opportunities for interesting work. It could be argued that the film falls into the 'Romance' category on the basis that the resolution is effected by the union of the initially mismatched leads, but there is another dimension to this film which could form the basis of some useful work on narrative.

Arguably, the main story arc is 'Phil's ordeal' and there is the sense that some force is at work which condemns him to repeat the same day until he learns how to live properly. Useful comparisons may be made with *It's a Wonderful Life* (Frank Capra, US, 1946), and, another Bill Murray vehicle, *Scrooged* (Richard Donner, US, 1988). In both these films, the protagonists learn to embrace life positively through the intervention of an angel and set of ghosts respectively, which force them to witness alternative unpleasant versions of reality. In *Groundhog Day* there is no angel, no ghost, no personified tormentor, but, nevertheless, a strong sense that Phil needs to mature, learn a lesson or be redeemed.

In addition to analysing *Groundhog Day* in terms of the Three Act Structure, students could use the Christopher Vogler approach to see if this illuminates the film in new ways. There could certainly be some useful debate about what constitutes 'The Ordeal' which, in Vogler's 'Central Crisis diagram' (*The Writer's Journey,* p161) occurs in the middle of Act II and in which the hero 'visits death' and may even appear to die. An obvious place to start is the montage sequence where Phil attempts to kill himself, but this occurs just over an hour into the film and is not, therefore, temporally central. Could it, then, be an example of 'Delayed Crisis' which, in an alternative schematic representation of the Three Act Structure, occurs later and 'allows a slow build-up to a big moment at the end of Act II'? (*The Writer's Journey,* p162) Or does this misunderstand the nature of 'The Ordeal' in *Groundhog Day*? His rejection by Rita occurs just after the halfway point – is this his ordeal?

The point is not to indulge in some kind of pseudo-scientific classification exercise, but to use paradigms and critical approaches to help students understand why something might be effective dramatically. If they understand why, there is a better chance of them being able to implement things which work equally well.

Character

Screenplays depend upon characters, as Syd Field says 'without character you have no action; without action, no conflict; without conflict, no story; without story, no screenplay.' (*The Screenwriter's Workbook*, p54)

We need to equip our students with some awareness of what makes a 'good' character and how to express this in a screenplay so that when they produce their own work it stands a much better chance of being original, imaginative and enjoyable.

Phil Parker suggests that all characters in any dramatic form have three essential aspects:

- Outer presence
- Inner presence
- Context

(*The Art and Science of Screenwriting,* pp 82–83)

The screenwriter, therefore, must consider, when constructing a character:

- The 'dominant impression' created by the character, dependent upon age, sex, mannerisms, physical appearance, clothes, grooming, movement, style of speech and so on.
- The 'dominant attitude' of the character, dependent upon their intelligence, knowledge, personality, temperament, likes/dislikes, beliefs, fears, goals, self-image, etc.
- The 'world' of the character, dependent upon relationships with friends, colleagues, lovers etc; their cultural background – class, education, where they were brought up, ethnicity; their general history – wartime or depression, for example; their personal history – significant events in the character's life, their personal 'back story'.

Worksheet 9

Students should be aware that a collection of attributes, like those above, do not necessarily make a compelling character and that, unless it is of narrative significance, the audience does not need to know that a character has a fear of ducks or loves the colour blue. However, it is useful to examine some introductions to characters from existing screenplays and evaluate them against the above lists and each other. The three examples in Worksheet 9 emphasise different aspects of character and the style of each is very different, but, of course, you can choose any examples you think will work well.

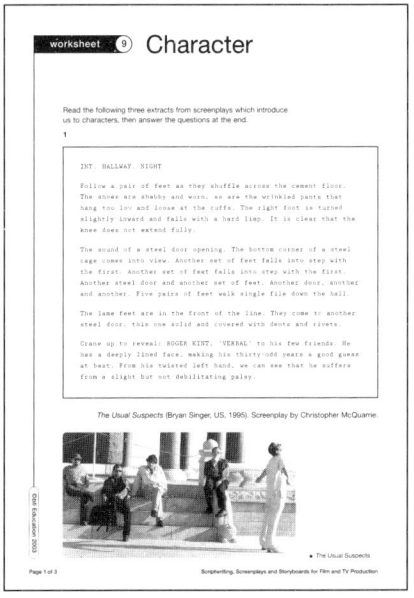

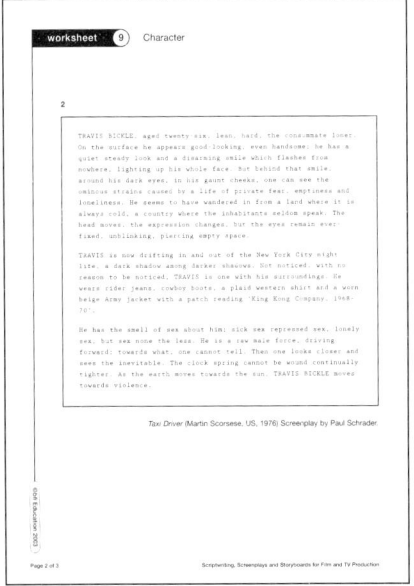

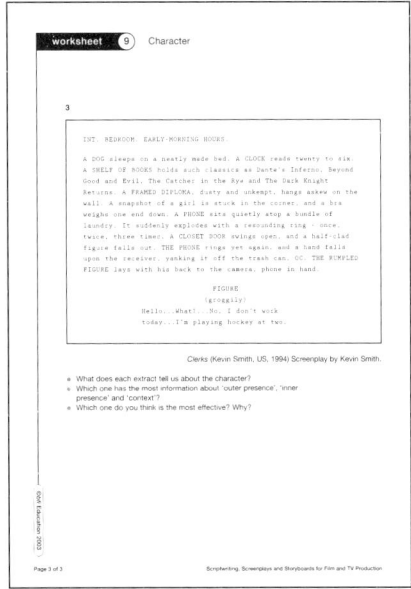

Worksheet 10

A good follow-up exercise is to ask students to create a character, to give them personal qualities, verbal tics and physical flaws and, if it is followed up by discussion, this can be a useful exercise. But more important than any list of attributes must be the way that a character acts in a crisis. In a screenplay, character is defined and revealed by action, so an interesting next step is for students to take their character and pursue, for example, questions about how that character would behave under pressure.

Encourage your students to generate and answer a range of questions (you could even use the regular Q&A feature in *The Guardian Weekend* magazine for ideas where questions include 'What is your idea of perfect happiness?' 'What is your greatest fear?' etc). The more answers students provide on behalf of their characters, the more these characters acquire emotional depth and the less likely they are to become caricatures or stereotypes. This can also be an excellent activity to generate story ideas at the start of a project, if needed.

Constructing dialogue and scenes

Before thinking analytically about screenplays it's easy to assume that they are mostly dialogue. In fact when discussing films it is common to hear people praising a 'script' when in fact they mean the dialogue. Our students are more likely to produce successful work if they understand the ways in which stories can be told through showing rather than telling, and if they realise that they can create impressive script and video work with little or no dialogue.

However, dialogue is an important component of the screenplay and it can be effective in student projects providing it is used with a specific purpose. Phil Parker suggests some qualities which characterise 'good dialogue' in a screenplay:

1 It has a clear dramatic function (eg to advance the story, reveal character).
2 It relates to the visual aspect of the moment (it should relate in some way to what we see on screen – it may be ironically juxtaposed against a setting, for example).
3 It is character-specific (a well-established test of this is to cover up the names in a screenplay and see if it is still clear who is speaking).
4 It is economical (in a realist drama, dialogue should be short and to the point).
5 It reflects the style of the narrative (the way that every character speaks should 'fit' the world they inhabit and should add to the rhythm and pace of the script).
6 It delivers only what the action and visuals cannot.
7 It is speech, not prose (it should convey the illusion of real speech, even though it is inevitably more structured).

(*The Art and Science of Screenwriting,* p178)

Raymond Frensham adds a list of 'don'ts':

1 Avoid 'passing-the-time-of-day' dialogue: greeting, polite nothings, goodbyes etc.
2 Don't repeat information in dialogue that has already occurred elsewhere in the dialogue.
3 Avoid dialect and writing phonetically: when the character is introduced, the description can contain information about accent, but script readers and actors don't like having to read phonetic representations of speech.

4 Never italicise dialogue to create emphasis and try to do it without exclamation marks.

5 Not every question asked in dialogue needs to be answered. The use of silence, a reaction or non-reaction can be as/more powerful than dialogue.

(*Teach Yourself Screenwriting,* p150)

These notes are available as a student handout at www.bfi.org.uk/tfms .

Worksheet 11

All instances of dialogue need to be understood in relation to their respective contexts, nevertheless, it is worth examining some short examples with students in order to highlight some of the points above. As mentioned elsewhere, it is better to look at screenplays which use standard format in order to create familiarity with the layout conventions. Worksheet 11 uses a short extract from Simon Beaufoy's script for *The Full Monty* (Peter Cattaneo, 1997, UK) which occurs shortly after the gang of aspiring strippers is arrested for indecent exposure during a practice session and usefully illustrates a number of points:

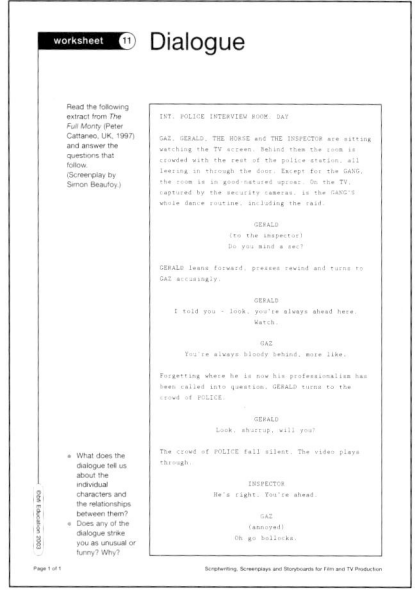

- It clearly relates to the visual situation and uses it to comic effect. The men have been arrested and are being presented with the evidence, yet their response, unexpectedly, is to use the video tape to provide evidence of flaws in the dance routine. In other words, the dialogue plays against the grain of the scene.
- It reveals character. The above juxtaposition between situation and response does not simply provide a joke which depends upon inappropriateness, it also reveals the extent to which (the initially reluctant) Gerald has been caught up in the desire to get it right. His commitment quells the troops and even pulls in an observation from the inspector. It also highlights the gentle antagonism between him and Gaz, the 'leader' of the gang.
- It avoids redundancy. We know why the men were 'exposing themselves' and we don't need to hear those arguments and justifications. Instead, Beaufoy creates dialogue for the men in which their 'innocence' of a crime is presented through their enthusiasm for the project.

- The dialogue represents speech. Vernacular voices are convincingly rendered, but, of course, artfully constructed, so that the inspector's words after a tangible pause fall like a punch line. This is economical writing, with no wastage (although, arguably, we could probably work out that Gaz delivers his last line in an 'annoyed' fashion).

Worksheet 12

A scene from *Good Will Hunting* (Gus Van Sant, 1996), in which the romantic leads meet for the first time, exemplifies another kind of writing, which could be described as more 'on the nose', in other words more straightforward with little sub-textual meaning. The scene, which follows one in which Will, the hero, has verbally humiliated an arrogant student for being wealthy and ignorant, can be contrasted with the more economical writing of *The Full Monty* scene.

Worksheet 13

A final example, the last scene in *Fargo* (Joel and Ethan Coen, 1996, US), can generate some useful debate around the use of more oblique dialogue. It's probably necessary to fill in the major story events which precede this scene, in which the heavily pregnant police officer, Marge, solves the case of a badly bungled kidnapping, which involves several murders and a body being fed into a wood-chipper. Although we have been made aware that the taciturn Norm has been painting birds and that there may be some kind of competition involved, we have not been told, until this point, why. Whether or not one feels that this scene 'works' in the context of the film, it is a good example of how to use dialogue which leaves much unstated and in which, although surface meaning is clear, there is a sense that the significance lies underneath.

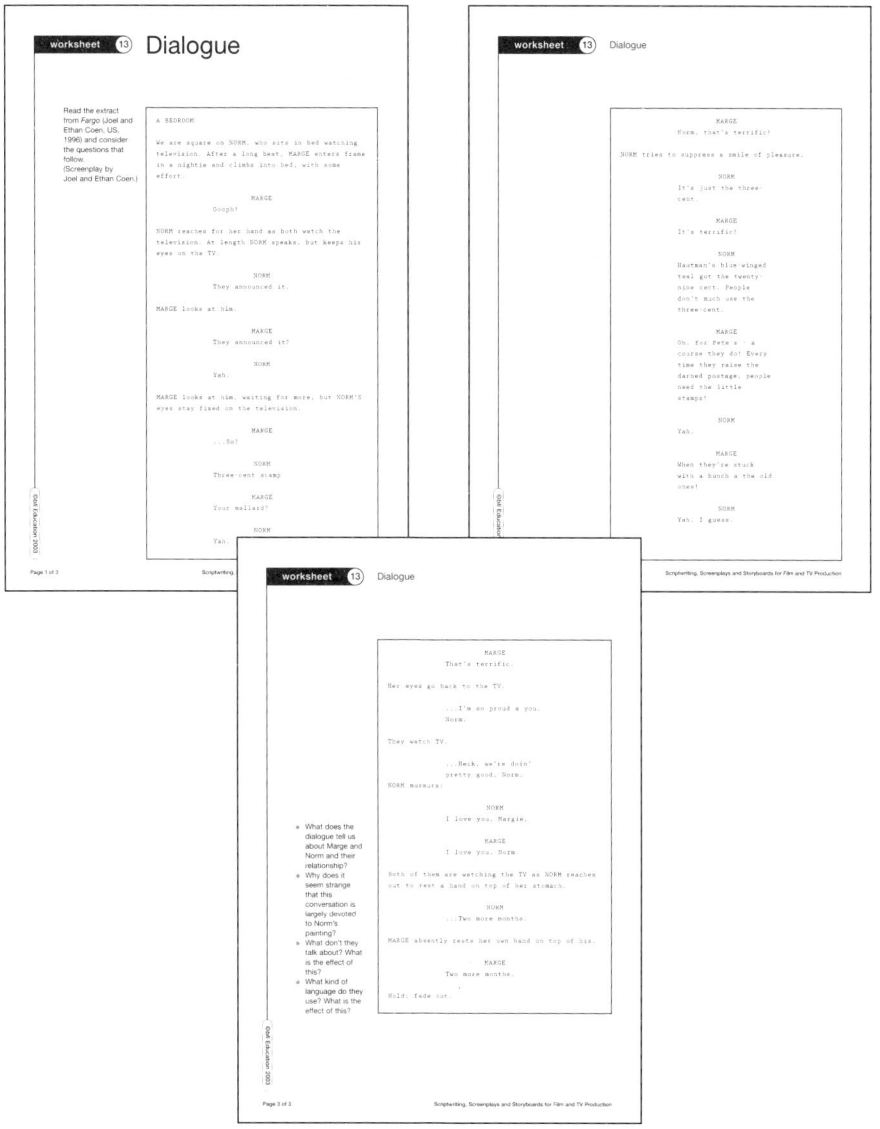

Worksheet 14

After studying these examples, in small groups or pairs students can practise writing dialogue in a controlled context. In Worksheet 14 students are presented with a range of scenarios, and asked to choose one and construct a scene based on it.

There is an opportunity as well here to discuss the function of scenes generally. Robert McKee argues that in every scene the 'value-charged condition of a character's life' should change, that is, from positive to negative or vice versa. He asserts:

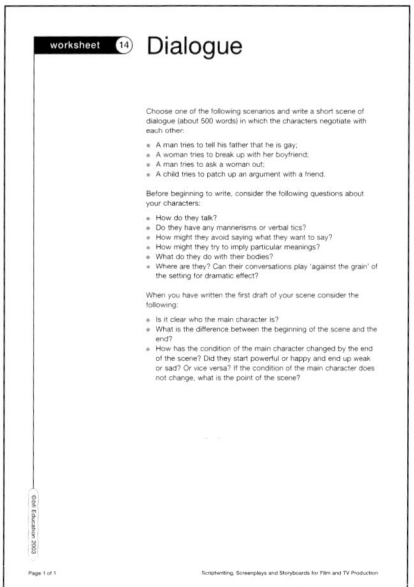

worksheet 14 Dialogue

Choose one of the following scenarios and write a short scene of dialogue (about 500 words) in which the characters negotiate with each other:

• A man tries to tell his father that he is gay;
• A woman tries to break up with her boyfriend;
• A man tries to ask a woman out;
• A child tries to patch up an argument with a friend.

Before beginning to write, consider the following questions about your characters:

• How do they talk?
• Do they have any mannerisms or verbal tics?
• How might they avoid saying what they want to say?
• How might they try to imply particular meanings?
• What do they do with their bodies?
• Where are they? Can their conversations play 'against the grain' of the setting for dramatic effect?

When you have written the first draft of your scene consider the following:

• Is it clear who the main character is?
• What is the difference between the beginning of the scene and the end?
• How has the condition of the main character changed by the end of the scene? Did they start powerful or happy and end up weak or sad? Or vice versa? If the condition of the main character does not change, what is the point of the scene?

Page 1 of 1   Scriptwriting, Screenplays and Storyboards for Film and TV Production

> 'if the value-charged condition of the character's life stays unchanged from one end of a scene to the other, nothing meaningful happens. The scene has activity – talking about this, doing that – but nothing changes in value. It is a non-event'. (*Story,* p36)

What might this mean in practice? Let's take one of the prescribed scenarios – 'a woman tries to break up with her boyfriend.' Perhaps at the beginning of the scene she feels in control, she's trying to let him down gently – this would be a positively 'value-charged condition'. But if, during the course of the scene, the boyfriend reveals that he is not going to let her go without a fight then she loses that control, she may even be fearful by the end of what he might do. Her 'value-charged condition' has changed to negative.

This is quite a challenge and, perhaps ought not to be introduced at the start of the exercise, but could be used to refine and improve the work being produced. McKee offers a detailed breakdown of a scene from *Casablanca* (Michael Urtiz, US, 1942) in order to illustrate exactly how this can work (*Story,* pp261–271).

It's worth noting here that McKee's definition of a scene is more of a dramatic than a technical one – 'the test of whether a series of activities constitutes a true scene is this: Could it have been written 'in one', in a unity of time and place?' (*Story,* p37) So the important point to note is that we do not necessarily expect to find a change in 'value' every time we cut to a different location. In a restaurant scene in *Don't Look Now* (Nicolas Roeg, UK/Italy, 1973), for example, there are technically seven scenes (we cut between the lavatory and the restaurant and there is a brief flashback). But there is only one story event – Laura's 'value-charged condition' changes from negative (enduring grief at the death of her daughter) at the beginning of the 'scene' to something else which may be 'positive' (delirium at the news that the spirit of her daughter is still present) at the end.

The results of the scene-writing exercise can be presented as dramatic readings – it takes the pressure off some students if there is the option of casting other people in their dramas – and the effectiveness of the dialogue discussed.

3

Storyboard basics

A storyboard is simply a sequence of drawings, similar to a comic book, which represents the sequence of shots in the finished screen-work. In addition to the drawings there is information about duration, sound effects, dialogue, the movement of objects within the frame and camera movement. In the real world, the storyboard is not the responsibility of the screenwriter, but is in the province of the director, who may work with a storyboard artist in order to realise a script visually. It is not necessarily a 'work of art' but it must be functional – essentially it must convey information about how the shots will be framed, how long they will last and how they will be sequenced. Consequently it is worth spending some time on prescriptive drawing and sequencing exercises.

Storyboarding can be laborious, and sometimes unpopular, but it does provide a useful training in visualisation and sequencing and is an essential part of the planning process. Fortunately there are now many examples of storyboards available both online (URLs in the bibliography, on page 77) and as extras on DVDs. For example, *Mission to Mars* (Brian De Palma, US, 2000) includes storyboards and animatics from key sequences in the film, and *Star Trek: The Motion Picture (The Director's Edition)* (Robert Wise, US, 1979) includes a storyboard archive.

Those with primitive drawing skills get easily disenchanted with the process of storyboarding and there are some common tendencies, such as:

- Using only one or a few frames to represent an entire scene;
- Failing to grasp that the storyboard frame represents the screen and drawing stick figures hanging in space;
- Avoiding the visual dimension altogether and writing descriptions in the frames.

If a storyboard is to be submitted as a final product there must be a high degree of correspondence between it and the moving image sequence it represents. If it is a step in the process of producing a piece of video work it must be a functional document which expresses narrative information visually. In either case it is important to highlight the skills that are necessary and practise them.

If hand-drawing storyboards is too difficult, digital photography can be a solution; but taking photographs should still be prefaced by mental visualisation and writing out a sequence of shots. Another solution is to use dedicated software, such as *StoryBoard Quick* which, although not cheap, enables the user to:

- Choose an aspect ratio for the frame;
- Select a location and background from an extensive library (or even import a digital image from another source);
- Select characters from the library in pre-drawn positions (additional character libraries, such as 'action' and 'ethnic' are available as extras);
- Select props and vehicles;
- Rotate, position and zoom characters;
- Add direction arrows and icons to indicate a dolly, zoom or tilt;
- Add captions;
- Re-shuffle the frames.

Version 3 even allows a script to be imported from a screenwriting program (including *Word*) and then sets up a new scene to be visualised for each slug line.

Storyboard Format

There is no single format used for storyboards. The template used in the examples in this pack includes space for essential information about sound, movement and duration and uses a screen ratio which approximates to the TV screen (1:33:1). Similar templates can easily be constructed using, for example, standard 'academy ratio' (1:85:1) or widescreen ratio (16:9) depending on what is required.

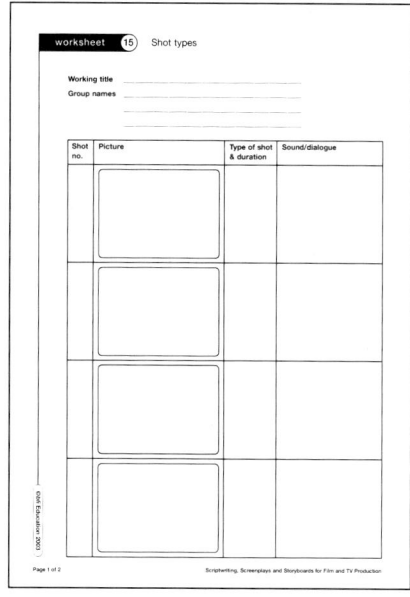

Shot types

Worksheet 15

● Activity 1

Initially it is worth establishing the vocabulary of shots, such as close up, establishing shot and high angle shot, for example. The function of different shot types should also be addressed – play a short sequence from a film or TV drama (muted) asking students to record the different shot types and then go through it again with the pause button and collate the responses. Almost anything will work for this exercise, providing there is an emphasis on visual information.

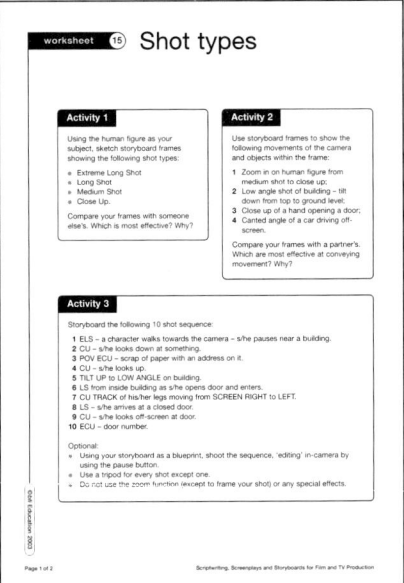

Worksheet 15, Activity 1 asks students to sketch specific shot types – an opportunity to address some technical as well as aesthetic issues – which may produce the results illustrated in figure 1. Even without highly developed drawing skills it is possible for students to create the illusion of depth using lines of perspective and, with some practice, effectively convey the human figure using simple shapes. This exercise can be enlivened by making a public activity out of it, using a whiteboard or flipchart and discussing why some shots perform some functions better than others.

When practising more difficult shot types, such as high and low angles, it can be useful to take appropriate shots using a video camera or a digital still camera and then to copy these into storyboard frames. Regular sessions of sketching practice can be scheduled in which students (and teachers, if necessary) establish some fairly simple techniques of conveying point of view and perspective in two dimensions.

| Working Title | | Page | I Of I |
| Group Names | | Date: | / / |

Shot No.	Picture	Type of shot & duration	sound/dialogue
		ELS	
		LS	
		MS	
	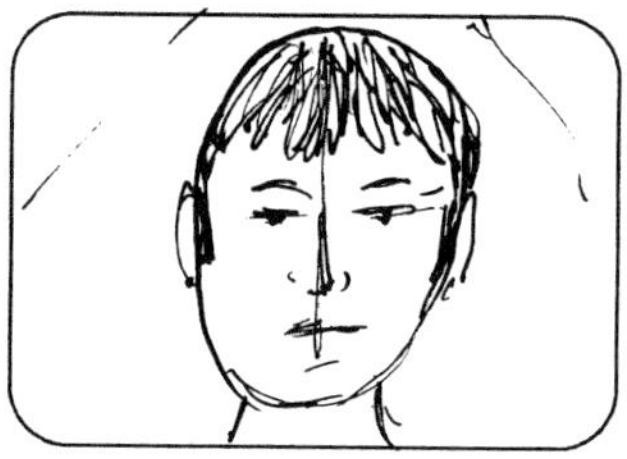	CU	

fig 1

Working Title	_____	Page	I Of I
Group Names	_____	Date:	/ /
	_____		
	_____		

Shot No.	Picture	Type of shot & duration	sound/dialogue
1	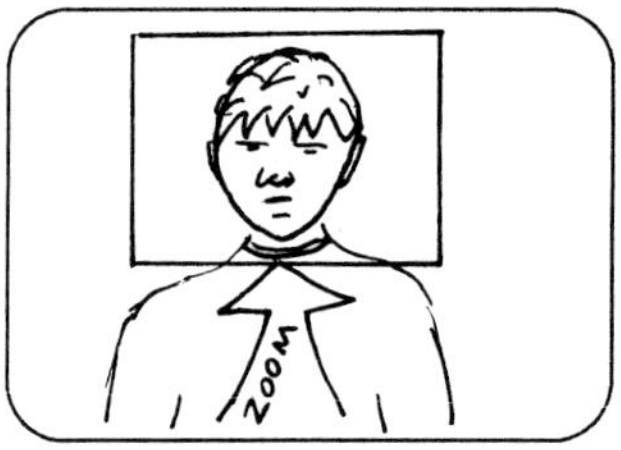	ZOOM IN TO C.U.	
2 ↓ ↓	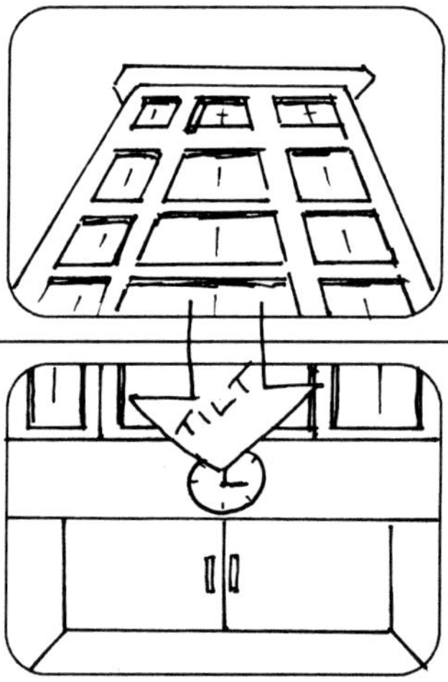	TILT DOWN FROM LOW ANGE ↓	
3		C.U. ON OPENING DOOR	

fig 2

● Activity 2

This exercise is primarily a technical one designed to get students to practise representing movement, of both the camera (in the form of zooms, tilts, pans and tracking shots) and objects within the frame. Essentially this entails the use of directional arrows and some simple preparatory demonstrations should help students. This is an opportunity to show how the frames of a storyboard can be used flexibly in order to 'animate' the sequence and movements and the possible outcomes of some of the examples in Worksheet 15 are illustrated below.

● Activity 3

This exercise builds upon skills of sketching and framing and develops an understanding of how shots can be simply sequenced to create narrative openings and enigmas. If this sequence can subsequently be shot and 'edited' in-camera by small groups it provides an excellent opportunity to exhibit and discuss the various versions that result. At the very least, the degrees of accuracy of framing can be discussed and, in addition, the effects of the different shot types can also be addressed. It can be useful to formalise a set of 'assessment criteria' for students to apply to each other's work, such as accuracy of framing, shot stability, shot duration and continuity as consideration of these can greatly benefit the 20-shot exercise which follows.

Worksheet 16

This exercise involves the creation of a storyboard sequence from an explicit list of visual events and should consolidate the previous work on framing and movement. The exercise is suited to group work, but the groups should be small enough to ensure that each member is involved in the construction of the storyboard. It also provides an opportunity for self-assessment if one is sufficiently confident to produce an 'authoritative version' and display it as an OHT. The illustration in fig 3 shows some of the shots that might result from Worksheet 16.

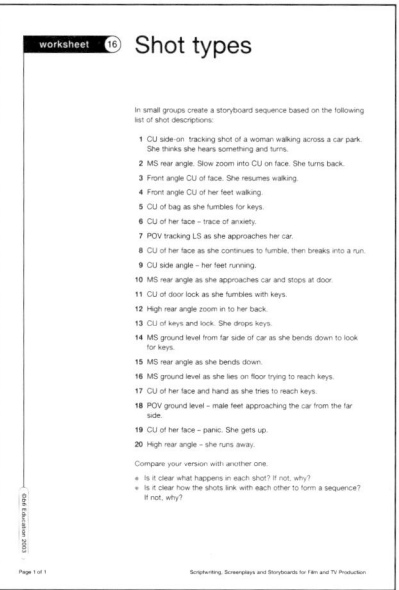

Working Title _____	Page ⏐ Of 3
Group Names _____	Date: / /
_____	
_____	

Shot No.	Picture	Type of shot & duration	sound/dialogue
1			
2			
3			
4			

fig 3 (i)

Working Title	_____	Page	2	Of 3
Group Names	_____	Date:	/	/
	_____			
	_____			

Shot No.	Picture	Type of shot & duration	sound/dialogue
5			
6			
7			
8			

fig 3 (ii)

Working Title _____		Page **3** Of **3**	
Group Names _____		Date: / /	
_____			
_____			

Shot No.	Picture	Type of shot & duration	sound/dialogue
9			
10			
11			
12			

fig 3 (iii)

The exercise can be extended into a video activity in which the small groups produce a video version of their storyboard which is 'edited' in camera. The advantage with this is that the shooting can be achieved in a short time (perhaps 30 minutes) and the results can be viewed immediately, stimulating discussion about the construction of narrative expectation through the vocabulary of available shots. There is another advantage to realising the sequence on video – the versions can be compared with the original, from which the above sequence has been transcribed (it is a short extract from an episode of *Buffy the Vampire Slayer*, Season 2, Episode 2 'Some Assembly Required'). This inevitably generates discussion about the importance of music and sound effects, the effects of different shot durations and camera movements and the quantity of shots used in such a short space of time. This is the kind of 'thriller' sequence that students may have otherwise been tempted to represent using one or two shots and this exercise demonstrates effectively how to generate tension through the fragmentation of space.

Sequencing

Worksheet 17

In a subsequent exercise students can build creatively on their awareness of framing and sequencing. Here, the requirement is for students to produce a storyboard of 15–20 shots in which they build up a sense of narrative expectation from a given scenario. You can invent your own scenarios, but some thought should be given to the objectives, which are to encourage students to do the following:

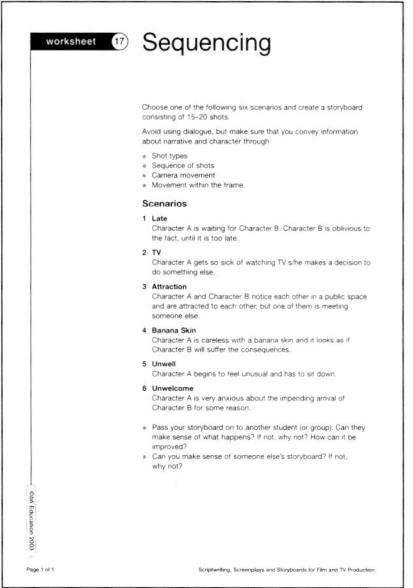

- Avoid simply assuming that the meaning of a scene is evident, or relying on making it apparent through dialogue.
- Establish a scene visually and then break it up into elements which have narrative significance.
- Use different shot types to convey information about character, mood and expectation.
- Use editing to establish relationships between characters and objects and create narrative expectation.

4

Planning a project

As has already been acknowledged, it is unlikely that our students will be required to write a feature-length screenplay, in fact it is more likely that they will be required to produce, for example:

- A screenplay extract of about 800 words;
- A complete screenplay for a short film of about 1800 words;
- A storyboard of about 20 shots representing a key moment in an imaginary film.

It is also likely that the work will need to be accompanied by some form of critical or explanatory commentary and a short synopsis. There may also be other requirements (to produce the opening of a thriller, for example).

Nevertheless, despite these constraints, there are many choices to be made and it can be valuable for students to go through specific planning stages as if they were producing a full length work, as this should maximise their potential for producing:

- Original (although maybe conventional) work, rather than work comprising parody, pastiche and cliché;
- Work which is fully contextualised and understood within a complete (and possibly complex) narrative framework;
- Work which is representative of something whole.

The stages in this section, then, lead students from conceptualising a complete narrative to planning a specific extract in screenplay or storyboard form.

If some or all of the activities described in Units 2 and 3 have been undertaken, there should be a reasonable degree of confidence with:

- The concept of screenplay structure;
- How to build logically coherent sequences of scenes and shots to construct a story;
- How dialogue might be used;
- How to convey character information and what kinds of stories exist to be told.

The challenge when beginning a project from scratch is not just to implement all of these elements, but also to develop an original idea. This section consists of a series of stages intended to plot the route from idea to finished product – either a storyboard or script extract.

The stages for presentation of work-in-progress and feedback on that work are designed to be opportunities for formative assessment – public and open spaces for dialogue and discussion about what works, what doesn't, what's appropriate, what isn't and so on. This should mean that we eliminate the possibility of students accepting an assignment brief, working in secret for a month and then submitting work which does not meet the requirements and subsequently receiving a disappointing grade for it.

Planning a project

Worksheet 18

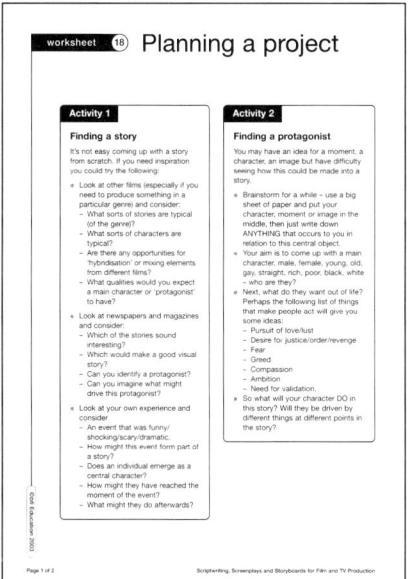
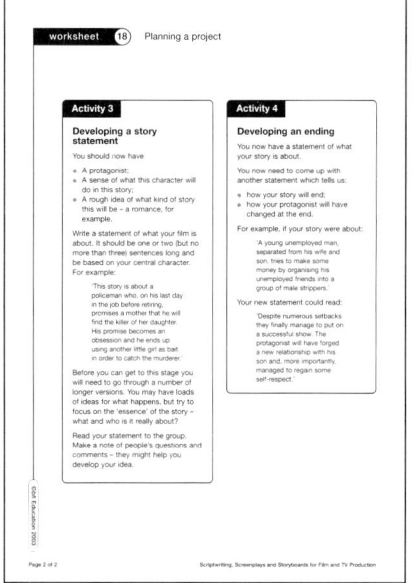

● Activity 1 – Finding a story

Assuming that the requirements of a specific assignment will take precedence, initially we need to suggest some ways of finding an idea. This activity contains a number of preliminary exercises which can be used to generate story ideas. These can be whole, small group or even individual activities.

● Activity 2 – Finding a protagonist

The second stage encourages students to brainstorm around whatever idea, however small, they have come up with and to develop its focus around a protagonist. Free association at this point is probably the best policy as it may result in some genuinely imaginative proposals. It may also be useful to revisit the character exercises in Unit 2.

● Activity 3 – Developing a story statement

Our aim at the next stage is to enable students to state that their story is about a particular character and a particular action. This only needs to be brief. Set a deadline by which each group or individual will publicly state what their story is about. If necessary, introduce a preliminary activity in which model statements are developed for existing films, eg:

'This story is about an anxious, claustrophobic single mother who discovers her inner strength when she has to protect her diabetic daughter when burglars break into their house.' *Panic Room* (David Fincher, US, 2002)

'This story is about a troubled psychiatrist with marriage problems, who, through his work with a boy who thinks he can see the dead, discovers that he is himself a ghost and reaches a kind of peace.' *The Sixth Sense* (M Night Shyamalan, US, 1999)

It's also worth using existing films to establish who the story is about; *Scream* (Wes Craven, US, 1996) for example, is not really about high school kids seeking revenge, but about Sidney Prescott's maturation and education – the Sidney at the end of the film is stronger, wiser and more resilient than the Sidney at the beginning.

● Activity 4 – Developing an ending

Despite the fact that a typical piece of assessed practical work is likely to be an extract from a whole (unless a short self-contained screenplay or film is being developed), it is important for students to know what the general shape of their stories will be like. This will ensure that their extract will be focused in narrative terms and its function will be unambiguous.

It may be useful to revisit some of the approaches discussed in Unit 2 in order to remind students of:

● The need for resolution;
● The nature of resolution (the notion of irreversible change);
● Different types of resolution (in relation to genre).

When 'ending statements' have been developed, it's worth creating a forum in which these can be read out – they should probably include the first statement as well, especially as this might have changed in the light of subsequent work. And, again, it's worth reminding students that feedback should be constructive and focused on story issues.

Establish some rules for the readings – make sure everyone understands that this is an early stage and that this is work in progress. Critical peer feedback can be valuable, but try to ensure that it is offered positively, perhaps suggesting some ways of beginning statements, like 'I think it would work even better if …'

Categorising the story

Worksheet 19

At this stage it's worth taking a step back in order to evaluate how the projects are progressing. Assessment so far has been peer-based, with the teacher occupying a co-ordinating role and retaining the ability to offer feedback where necessary. It is possible now for students briefly to assess the success of the progress of their own work in relation to some of the models offered earlier. This exercise can take as little as 15 minutes, but is a valuable opportunity for reflection.

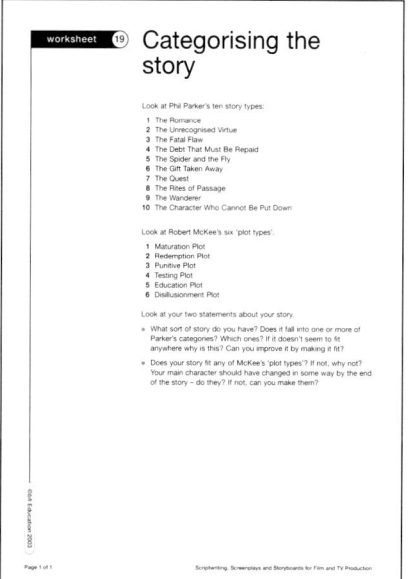

Structuring the story

Worksheet 20

It is appropriate now to move towards organising the story using the Three Act Structure. Worksheet 20 asks students to use the Three Act Structure diagram to map out their story.

Make it clear that, at this stage, students do not need to know every detail, but that, by the end of the exercise, they should know roughly:

- What will be established in Act I;
- What will happen in Act II;
- What will happen in Act III;
- What the turning points are towards the end of Act I and Act II respectively.

This task can be assessed via presentation and verbal feedback again, but given the importance of establishing these story struts, you may like to take in the documents and offer written feedback.

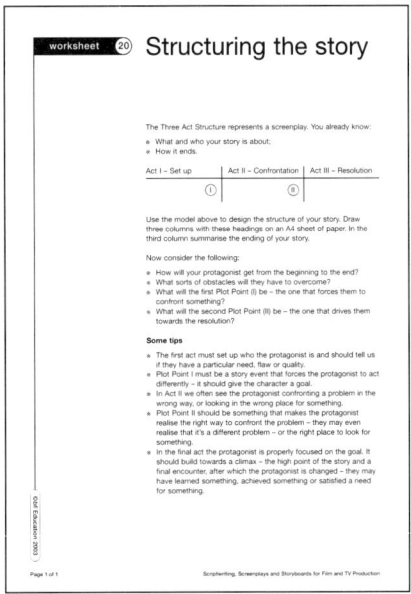

Developing a treatment and a pitch

Worksheet 21

● Activity 1 – A treatment

'Treatment' is a term which is used to mean various things, some of which are also referred to as the 'outline' or 'synopsis'. Phil Parker differentiates between the 'full treatment', which may be 10–20 pages or more, and the short, four-page, treatment which he calls an 'outline'. Syd Field also discusses the merits of the 'four-page treatment' and, for our purposes, given the likely outcomes of this work, four pages seems more than adequate (in fact, two to four pages would probably suffice) and we shall stick with the term 'treatment'. If the

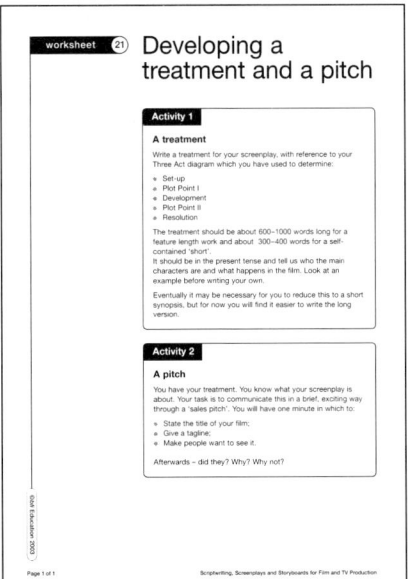

final product is to be a self-contained short film, a shorter treatment will be enough. If necessary the treatment can be used as the basis for an abbreviated synopsis of 200 words or so.

The treatment should be a present tense prose version of the intended screen story and should establish:

- The main characters and their motivation;
- A clear dramatic structure;
- The essential narrative events, including the resolution of the main story or stories.

Ideally, the style of the treatment should reflect the style of the screenplay – many see it as a 'written pitch' – although this is difficult to achieve in the shorter format.

An example of a treatment for a 10-minute 'short' is given in the **Appendix**.

Having a forum for individuals and groups to read out their treatments is a great opportunity for instant feedback, but it can become tedious if the treatments are all lengthy. Alternatively, the treatments can be photocopied and passed around. Students can be encouraged to offer brief written comments. It is a good idea to provide guidelines for these, suggesting that comments focus on narrative coherence, character motivation and the strength of Plot Points.

● Activity 2 – A pitch

An alternative to reading out the treatments can be to give a verbal 'pitch'. This is a useful way of clarifying and condensing the story and it can also clarify the notional audience for the work and the genre. At the very least there is an opportunity here to discuss the effects of titles and the function of taglines. For example, you could ask what is suggested by the title *Unbreakable* (M Night Shyamalan, US, 2000) and how this is inflected by the tagline, 'Are you ready for the truth?' If necessary, students could create pitches for existing films (it may or may not be a good idea to offer scenes from *The Player* (Robert Altman, US, 1992) as examples of how to pitch!). Worksheet 21, Activity 2 includes some suggestions.

Developing a sequence

Worksheet 22

● Activity 1 – A script

Armed with a treatment, which details the dramatic structure of the narrative (which, conceivably, might feature a number of stories), it should be possible for students to make an informed choice about which part of the narrative they will script. This choice can be made through consultation with a teacher and/or through dialogue with peers, but it should be clear that it makes sense to opt for a turning point, a climax or a dramatic opening. It may be useful to revisit some of the exercises in Unit 2, particularly those which look at how to communicate information visually and through dialogue.

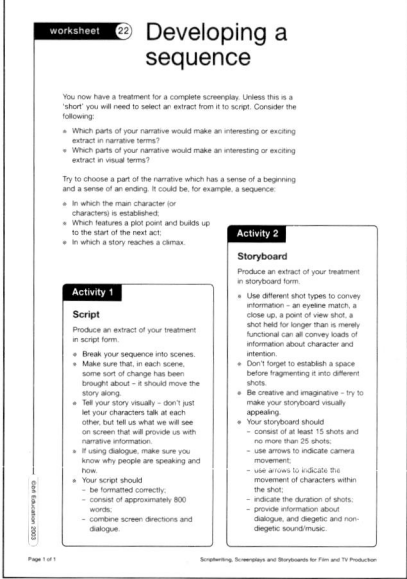

A coursework assignment will have specific requirements so the guidelines in Worksheet 22 will need to be contextualised accordingly.

● Activity 2 – A storyboard

As with the development of a script extract it is important for a storyboard extract (which is likely to consist of about 20 shots) to represent a key moment in the narrative. In addition to this, it is important for a moment to be selected which offers a high degree of visual interest so that students can demonstrate their ability to manipulate the form effectively.

It may be useful to revisit some of the practical exercises in Unit 3 in order to revise ways of creating frames and sequences.

Glossary

Beat
Directional word used to indicate a pause in an actor's speech or action of a sequence.

Camera angle
The position of the frame in relation to the subject it shows: looking down (high angle), on the same level (straight-on angle) or looking up (low angle).

Canted angle (also known as Dutch angle)
Shot in which the horizontal frame line is not parallel to the horizon.

Close-up
Shot in which the subject is larger than the frame – approximately from the top of the chest to the top of the head.

Continuity
The continuous flow of a film/TV programme where shot follows shot in a smooth understandable way. Effective continuity is dependent upon the logical matching of details, movement and dialogue from shot to shot and makes us unaware of the *cutting*.

Contra zoom
An effect created by tracking in and zooming out, or tracking out and zooming in. The subject in the foreground maintains its position within the frame, yet the background changes, thus causing a disorienting effect.

Cut
The instantaneous change from one shot to another.

Diegesis
In a narrative film (or TV programme), the world of the film's story. The diegesis includes events, actions and spaces which are not necessarily shown on screen.

Diegetic sound
Any voice, musical sound or sound effect presented as originating from a source within the film's world. ***Non-diegetic* sound**, therefore, includes such elements as mood music and a narrator's commentary because they do *not* have a source within the fictional world of the film.

Dissolve (also known as **mix**)
A transition between two shots whereby the first gradually fades out as the second gradually fades in. The technique can be used to create various meanings, eg a slow dissolve can be used to suggest the passage of time between two scenes.

Editing
The entire process of assembling a film or TV product, which includes the selection and sequencing of shots, the arrangement of scenes and the integration of soundtracks.

Establishing shot
Usually a long, wide shot showing much of the location, intended to prime the audience for an imminent scene.

Insert
Close-up shot of an object in the context of a scene.

Jump cut
Cut which interrupts the continuity of time.

Medium shot
Camera angle often used to describe a shot of a figure from the waist up.

Mise en scène
All the elements placed in front of the camera to be filmed – the settings and props, lighting, costumes, make up and actions of characters. *Mise-en-scéne* analysis examines how the arrangement of these elements creates particular meanings.

OS (Off screen)
An indication in a screenplay (in brackets after the character's name) that, although the character is present in the scene, they are not visible. Not be used in the same way as VO (voice over).

Pan
A camera movement along a horizontal axis, with the camera body turning the left or right on a stationary tripod.

Prop
Object on the set used by an actor, such as phones, guns or cutlery.

Point of view shot (POV shot)
A shot taken with the camera placed approximately where the character's eyes would be, showing what the character would see; usually cut in before or after a shot of the character looking off screen.

Reaction shot
Shot of person reacting to dialogue or action.

Slug line
A header appearing in a script before each scene detailing the location and time.

Synchronous sound
The placement of sound so that it seems to come directly from some action within the image, eg, dialogue corresponding to lip movements.

Tilt

A camera movement along a vertical axis, with the camera body swivelling up or down on a stationary tripod.

Tracking shot

Any shot in which the camera body moves, often on a wheeled support (or **dolly**), forwards, backwards or laterally.

VO (Voice over)

An indication in a screenplay (in brackets after a character's name) that a character's (or narrator's) voice only is present. Unlike an off-screen (OS) voice, this is non-diegetic (it does not exist within the fictional world of the film) and is addressed to the audience.

Whip pan

Extremely fast pan, incorporating motion blur.

Wipe

A transition between two shots whereby the second gradually appears by pushing or 'wiping' off the first.

Zoom

Shot in which the magnification of the objects by the camera's lenses is increased (zoom in) or decreased (zoom out).

This glossary is available as a student handout at www/bfi.org.uk/tfms.

Appendix

Fast Forward
A treatment for a sci-fi short

London. The present. John Foster is 26 and a scientist. He works in a lab for a pharmaceutical company in their research division. It's fairly routine work but he has a laugh with his good friend Simon, a technician at the lab, and at the weekends they party on the various 'designer drugs' that John synthesises in his spare time. At work Simon flirts effortlessly with Sarah, a fellow technician, and it becomes clear that John is rather infatuated with her. Simon encourages him to ask her out, but John is still, at heart, the geeky science kid from school and is too inhibited.

One evening, working late and pursuing his illicit career as 'alchemist of consciousness', John stumbles across a kind of 'hyper amphetamine' which accelerates the entire metabolism to hundreds, maybe thousands of times more than normal. For the user, the world appears to slow down almost to a standstill so that, whereas they may experience ten minutes, only a second or so has elapsed in reality.

Excited by the discovery, John visits Simon and they take the drug together. Out on the street the world, stalled in time, becomes their playground and they play pranks on passersby. John, intoxicated with the experience declares from the roof of a car that they are 'gods'. Suddenly the drug begins to wear off, the world begins to come to life again and with it come cramps and nausea for John and Simon.

The next day John suggests a repeat performance that evening, but Simon regretfully declines – he's meeting an old friend. Later, on his way home, John notices Sarah going into a bar. He girds his loins and follows her in but loses the courage to approach her once inside. However, he realises that he could get closer if he takes the new drug. He takes some in the lavatory and, at the motionless bar starts to tell Sarah how he feels, but then follows her eyeline and realises that she is greeting Simon! Confused and feeling a bit betrayed,

John then has to deal with the comedown from the drug, which is significantly worse than before.

John now becomes more withdrawn and secretive. He uses the drug to spy on Simon and Sarah, obsessively analysing their body language as if they were statues and becomes convinced that they are lovers. His withdrawals from the drug become progressively worse.

Finally he confronts Simon, accusing him of stealing Sarah behind his back. Simon denies this, telling John that he was simply putting in a good word for him. He realises that John's dependency on the drug has become total and, when John collapses, has to administer a dose to his friend in order to save his life.

At the end we hear John, in voice over, tell us that, far from being a 'god', he is now trapped in this world of statues. We see his lonely existence in a silent, still world. A final close-up shows a much older, haggard John kissing Sarah, but it is revealed that she is making love with Simon. John tells us that one day he might have the courage to 'let go', but not yet.

This appendix is available as a student handout at www/bfi.org.uk/tfms.

Bibliography

- **Books (Screenwriting)**

R A Blum, 1995, *Television and Screenwriting: From Concept to Contract* (3rd edition), Focal Press.

S Field, 1984, *The Screenwriter's Workbook*, Dell.

S Field,1994, *Four Screenplays*, Dell.

S Field, 1994, *Screenplay* (3rd edition), Dell.

R G Frensham, 1996, *Teach Yourself Screenwriting*, Hodder & Stoughton.

J Friedmann and P Roca (eds), 1994, *Writing Long-Running Television Series*, Media Business School.

W Goldman, 2000, *Which Lie Did I Tell? More Adventures in the Screen Trade*, Bloomsbury.

R Harmon, 1988, *Film Producing: Low Budget Films that Sell*, Samuel French Trade.

R McKee, 1998, *Story*, Methuen.

A Owen (ed), 2000, *Smoking in Bed: Conversations with Bruce Robinson*, Bloomsbury.

P Parker, 1999, *The Art and Science of Screenwriting* (2nd edition), Intellect.

W Smethurst, 2000, *Writing for Television* (3rd edition), How To Books.

E Vale, 1998, *Vale's Technique of Screen and Television Writing* (Revised edition), Focal Press.

C Vogler, 1999, *The Writer's Journey: Mythic Structure for Storytellers and Screenwriters* (2nd edition), Pan.

J Wolff, 1996, *Successful Sitcom Writing* (2nd edition), St Martin's Press.

• Books (Storyboards)

J O Fraioli, 2000, *Storyboarding 101: A Crash Course in Professional Storyboarding*, Michael Wiese Productions.

J Hart, 1999, *The Art of the Storyboard: Storyboarding for Film, TV and Animation*, Focal Press.

S D Katz, 1991, *Film Directing Shot by Shot*, Michael Wiese Productions.

M Simon, 2000: *Storyboards, Motion in Art* (2nd edition), Focal Press.

• Screenplays (with publication dates – not film release dates)

S Beaufoy, 1997, *The Full Monty*, Screenpress Books.

E and J Coen, 1996, *Fargo*, Faber and Faber.

M Damon and B Affleck, 1998, *Good Will Hunting*, Faber and Faber.

C McQuarrie, 1996, *The Usual Suspects*, Faber and Faber.

P Schrader, 1990, *Taxi Driver*, Faber and Faber.

K Smith, 1997, *Clerks & Chasing Amy*, Faber and Faber.

• Journals

Screentalk (6 issues per year, info at www.screentalk.org)

Script Writer (6 issues per year, info at www.scriptwritermagazine.com)

Creative Screenwriting (6 issues per year, info at www. creativescreenwriting.com)

• Websites

http://www.scifi.com/exposure/frameup/joyride.html
View Jim Gillespie's *Joyride* online

http://imdb.com/
The internet movie database – great for dates, blurbs, casts and taglines.

www.script-o-rama.com
Hundreds of film and TV scripts and transcripts which can be downloaded.

http://shootingpeople.org/
Register here to get emailed bulletins (still free if you opt for the digest every three days) about screenwriting – often interesting debates, questions, answers and arguments about writing and writers.

http://www.premiere.com/Premiere/Features/Hannibal/storyboards.html
A selection of storyboards from *Hannibal* (Ridley Scott, 2001, US)

http://marsattacks.warnerbros.com/cmp/1-storyboards.html
A selection of storyboards from *Mars Attacks!* (Tim Burton, 1996, US)

http://www.stargate-sg1.com/home/behind/storyboards.html
A selection of storyboards from *Stargate SG1* (MGM TV, 1997 -)

http://www.tron-movie.com/production/Storyboards/
A selection of storyboards from *Tron* (Steven Lisberger, 1982, US)

http://spideymovie.20m.com/storyboards.html
A selection of storyboards from *Spiderman* (Sam Raimi, 2002, US)

These links are available through www.bfi.org.uk/tfms .

● DVDs (containing storyboards as 'extras')

Mission to Mars (Brian De Palma, US, 2000)

Star Trek: The Motion Picture (The Director's Edition) (Robert Wise, US, 1979)

Notes

Notes

Notes

Notes

Notes

Notes